Love, Lori Sato

SHE
IS
ME

SHE IS ME

HOW WOMEN WILL SAVE THE WORLD

LORI SOKOL, PhD

SHE WRITES PRESS

Published 2020

ISBN: 978-1-63152-715-9
ISBN: 978-1-63152-716-6
Library of Congress Control Number: 2020904740

For information, address:
She Writes Press
1569 Solano Ave #546
Berkeley, CA 94707

Interior design by Tabitha Lahr

She Writes Press is a division of SparkPoint Studio, LLC.

To my daughter, Rebecca, who serves as my perpetual sounding board, and who often knows me better than I know myself.

To my son, Jason, and his husband, Olivier, who live with complete honesty and respect for human rights and the sustainability of our planet.

To Brooke Warner and She Writes Press, for guiding and supporting me throughout this book writing process.

And to all of the women who have believed in me unconditionally, freeing me to become all that I am capable of, especially:

Loreen Arbus
Amy Ferris
Rudrani
Lillian Spin
Gloria Steinem

I am possible because of you.

CONTENTS

FOREWORD

*"I would say that each of us has only one
thing to gain from the feminist movement:
Our whole humanity, because gender has wrongly
told us that some things are masculine, and some
things are feminine . . . which is bullshit."*

—GLORIA STEINEM, author and activist

When I was five, I wanted to die. I was lying on the plastic-covered living room couch. It was a sixties thing—wrapping couches and chairs entirely in plastic to prevent the furniture below from showing signs of wear. It also blocked any feelings of warmth or comfort emanating from the soft fabric inside.

It was a hot, sweaty summer day. No air conditioners were allowed in the Brooklyn, New York, public housing complex where my parents, my older brother, and I shared a small two-bedroom apartment. One large gray fan stood in the middle of the living room, circulating warm air in one direction. Still, I wrapped my entire body in a blanket. It felt somewhat safer inside a cocoon-like covering; encased, protected. While watching a cartoon on the black-and-white television set a few feet away, I stopped breathing. I did not move or call out for help, however. *Finally, peace,* I thought. I gently closed my eyes.

The terrorist I lived with was standing no more than ten feet away, in the kitchen. As a father, his temper flared almost daily and spontaneously. My only warning sign was a behavior that was very confusing to others, but for my mother, brother, and me, it was all too familiar. He would stick out his tongue just far enough to protrude outside his mouth, immediately roll it underneath into a ball, and then harshly bite down on it with his upper teeth. Instantaneously, I responded by turning my back to him in hopes of lessening the pain from the physical blows that followed. He always used his right hand, his fist landing mostly on the left side of my head.

My father must have found me lying alone on the couch that day, not breathing. I don't know how, exactly, since I had fallen unconscious, and reopened my eyes to find him with me in the back seat of a taxi taking us to the closest hospital. I was ultimately diagnosed with bronchial pneumonia, remaining in the hospital for eight days. Once the x-rays showed that the pneumonia cleared my lungs, I returned home . . . to *his* home. The hospital, which had served as a safe respite, now faded from view.

The blows I suffered from my father were never warranted. Truly, how could any parent hitting a child ever be warranted, since it always has more to do with the abuser than the young and innocent victim? But he always found a reason that made sense only to him, whether it was because I spoke too loudly, cried too deeply, or breathed incorrectly. "Stop breathing with your stomach going in and out instead of up and down, or else you'll get a fat stomach!" he'd yell. A strong man, a "macho" man, who was compared by many who knew him to Jack LaLanne, the American fitness, exercise, and motivational speaker often referred to as the First Fitness Superhero of the 1960s and '70s, my father was also named Jack, and often referred to as a "hero" and "legend" by friends and neighbors. He was admired for his ability to run and complete marathons until the age of sixty-five, yet our family superhero was also paralyzed by the most mundane things—unwilling or unable to drive a car, correctly dial a rotary telephone, or properly use a paper clip. These lapses, which reflected basic abilities for most, kept him guarded and scared. His fear of being exposed and humiliated compelled him to control those closest to him by abusing and belittling us, all to help reduce his inner feelings of insecurity and shame.

Patriarchy not only befitted him, it engulfed him, providing the ultimate mask to conceal his failings, while justifying his violent outbursts to keep those closest to him diminished. Females, he believed, were secondary citizens, alive only to serve as his punching bag, his doormat. It was a belief my older brother, Kevin, learned from him all too well. It is not uncommon for physical aggression and antisocial behavior to occur among childhood victims of physical abuse, since they learn to view such behavior as an appropriate means of resolving conflict. So, my brother projected his failures—mounting ones at school and in sports—onto me as well. But he used his left hand as well as his right, pushing me into tables, doors, and chairs; anything with a sharp edge.

My mother sometimes came to my rescue, but only slightly and temporarily. Handing me a handkerchief filled with ice cubes to place over the ensuing swelling appearing just above my eyes, she made me remove it before my father returned home from work. "Don't let your father see," she warned me. Her first priority was to protect my brother. This is common for wives of domestic abusers who have internalized their misogyny, protecting the (often male) abuser over the (often female) victim.

Still, my mother did provide me with some hope to have a better life—once I became an adult, that is. In fact, she named me *Lori* to help ensure I would. My name was meant to bring me luck, but not just any kind of luck, like being born with intelligence, or with a musical, artistic, or athletic talent, or with any other quality that could help me achieve independently in life. No, the only luck my mother could possibly envision for me would come from someone else: a man. Lori was the name of the lead actress in the popular 1950s television series, *How to Marry a Millionaire*. By naming me Lori, she hoped that I, too, would grow up to marry a wealthy man, since she had not. What she refused to acknowledge, however, was that it wasn't being married to money that mattered most, but being married to a man who didn't abide by the patriarchal rules of power and dominance over his wife and children.

The first time I became acutely aware of the extreme gender inequality in our home was when I was seven years old, during the first month of second grade. My teacher recommended to the school principal that I skip second grade and move immediately into third. This would place me in the same grade as my brother. "How would that look?" my father nervously responded, while my mother adamantly refused, warning me, "You're not going to think you are better than anyone else!" The older I got, the worse it became. Since I didn't fit neatly into the stereotypical feminine box of playing with dolls, wearing ribbons in my hair, or being "seen and not heard," I was punished when I brought home good grades at the end of each school year and my brother did not. When I won trophies for my athletic prowess, I was told to hide them. Rather than acting out in protest, however, I hunkered down until I was old enough to move out. And when I finally did, after graduating from college at the early age of twenty, I devoted my career to helping others, particularly women and girls who are also experiencing similar feelings of loneliness and isolation living within the strict confines of an abusive patriarchal society. As a passionate writer, I chose to do so as a journalist, where I could reach many more women and girls, through both my observations and my words.

Writing, after all, had always served as my lifeline throughout those traumatic childhood years. My personal journal, which I wrote in daily, was my one trusted friend, a place where I could express my feelings, hopes, and goals secretly and without judgment. Embarking on a career in journalism, I hoped to serve as a live personal journal whom other women could trust to express themselves freely, and without fear.

And that's what led me to write this book. In interviewing countless highly accomplished women for over three decades, there have been some common threads, recurring qualities and values that each exhibited, regardless of their chosen fields. Whether it was Gloria Steinem, the iconic feminist, author, and human rights activist; Billie Jean King, the women's tennis champion once ranked best in the world; Sarah Ferguson, the Duchess of York, who turned oppressive insults about her weight into helping others embrace their bodies at whatever size; or Leymah Gbowee, the 2011 Nobel Peace Laureate and Liberian peace activist—each exhibited warmth, compassion, and humility. Yet, these virtues were not exhibited only behind closed doors. They utilized their tools for success to enable countless others to reach their full potential and even, in some cases, save their lives. That brought me to wonder whether other highly accomplished women possessed the same or similar qualities, and how these qualities had proven helpful to empower and save others as well. Further, could these qualities, if put to work on a grander scale, resolve our world's most crucial challenges, like preventing or ending war, and eradicating climate change, thereby ensuring a safer, healthier, and more peaceful world for future generations? We are currently living in a pivotal time in history, where the fear of losing long-held patriarchal control is causing members of marginalized groups (including women, the LGBTQ community, people of color, and people with disabilities) to be scapegoated and physically attacked. Further, patriarchy's refusal to accept glaring facts about climate change is threatening our planet's long-term survival.

In the pages that follow, you will not only be taken inside the private homes, offices, and classrooms of each of these five women who gave rise to this book, but also twenty-five others who have since been interviewed, including authors, actors, film-makers, philanthropists, and political leaders, to learn how they are successfully dedicating their work, and their lives, for the greater good of all. They will further demonstrate how being able to freely display values that exist in all of us—empathy, modesty, compassion, warmth, and introspection—will not only free us universally, but will also provide us with what may be our very last chance to save the world.

Five who gave rise to this book:

SARAH FERGUSON, DUCHESS OF YORK

"I learn as much from others as they learn from me."

—SARAH FERGUSON, Duchess of York

I t is the stuff of fairytales. A girl born into a family of modest means grows up to marry a real prince. He proposes by presenting her with an extravagant engagement ring: custom-designed with a Burma ruby (to match her red hair), surrounded by ten drop diamonds. Just two months later, they marry in a palatial wedding at London's Westminster Abbey, one of the most historic and monumental buildings in the world. They exchange wedding rings, crafted from Welsh gold, in tradition with his royal family's supreme lineage. The wedding cake, rum-soaked and made of marzipan, stands over five feet tall. There are two, in fact, just in case one gets damaged as it's transported to the wedding reception, where two thousand friends and family members await their arrival. An additional five hundred million people from around the world tune in to watch Prince Andrew, Duke of York, marry Sarah Ferguson in 1986, witnessing the bride's vow to "love, cherish, and obey" her husband. She stands at the altar, shrouded in purity and conviction, in an elaborately designed white silk wedding dress, a seventeen-foot train, and a twenty-foot-long veil. A diamond tiara, gifted to her just minutes earlier by her soon-to-be mother-in-law, Queen Elizabeth, sits stiffly atop her head. "I had to quickly lose twenty-four pounds just to fit into that dress," Sarah was quoted as saying at the time.

It was now 2004, eight years after the royal couple's divorce, when I interviewed Sarah Ferguson. She was serving as the ambassador and national spokesperson for Weight Watchers, the global weight-loss company hailed not only for helping people shed unwanted pounds, but also for encouraging healthy eating. Perhaps Sarah took on this role because she had been cruelly and relentlessly labeled the "Duchess of Pork" and "Fat Frumpy Fergie" by the tabloids when she was unable to lose the weight she gained after giving birth to each of her two daughters. Or perhaps it was because she wanted to take her weight control goals into her own hands rather than to be incessantly victimized by the British press and others. I suspect it was both.

As the founder and publisher of *Work Life Matters* magazine, a national publication I launched in 2002 to advocate for flexibility, diversity, and wellness in the workplace, I was offered a personal interview with Sarah. It was just a few weeks after I had interviewed New York University Medical Center's senior human resources staff for a feature article about their pioneering dedication to the health and wellness of their employees. Including information about Sarah Ferguson's upcoming appearance at the medical center to discuss her successful weight loss through Weight Watchers, a program the medical center also offered to its employees, would augment their article nicely, they suggested when they pitched me the idea. I agreed.

Sarah spoke on stage to a packed auditorium of hundreds of employees who were also Weight Watchers' clients. Demonstrating her compassion and empathy for the similar struggles of others, she shared stories about her previous dieting disasters, including once tipping the scale at over two hundred pounds, only to lose the added weight and then balloon up again by finding solace in a mixture of "sausages and mayonnaise," she confided on stage. After finishing her speech, she devoted the remaining time to questions from the audience. Those who stepped up to the microphone did not ask questions, however. Instead they all revealed their own weight loss struggles and triumphs, some of them expressing their sublimated fears of reverting back to dangerous eating habits. Tears were shed amid spontaneous rounds of applause for the courage each displayed in sharing their intimate stories. "I learn as much from others as they learn from me," Sarah told me later during our interview.

After she stepped off stage, we rode the elevator together up to a private room to conduct her interview. Once the security guard closed the door behind us, she, her bodyguard, and I sat down around a circular white table. A small plate of food was placed before her. "Do you mind if I eat while we talk," she asked me, "I haven't eaten all day."

Relieved to see how informal she was, I responded in kind. "Of course," I said, as I leaned back in my chair, making myself comfortable. I immediately thought, *She feels comfortable enough to eat in front of me.* It felt intimate to me, given all that my profession had put her through. *This is going to be an engaging and insightful interview.*

In person, Sarah appeared much more striking than I had ever seen her in magazine photos, or even on the television screen. Her sparkling blue eyes dominate. Her red hair radiates. But on this day, her dazzling features were juxtaposed against a conservative and understated navy-blue skirt suit, starkly contrasted by a pair of brightly colored turquoise stockings. I wondered about this unusual color choice but dared not mention it. *Perhaps it was some kind of new British fashion trend*, I thought.

Sarah did not waste any time addressing exactly what I was thinking. "You're probably wondering why I chose to wear turquoise stockings with this suit," she asked, her blue eyes now focused more intently. "Well, when I opened the closet door in my hotel room this morning and saw these stockings, I thought, *No one would dare wear turquoise stockings with a navy-blue suit,* so I did. This shows that I no longer care about what other people think of me," she said proudly. She then pointed to the black-and-white cowgirl boots I was wearing, offsetting my all-black pantsuit. "You see, you're wearing this solid black suit, and most women would just wear black shoes to match, but you took a risk by going with those."

As we carried on, we discovered that defying fashion norms was not the only thing we had in common. In fact, this defiance was actually a reflection of similar experiences as children of parents who did not provide us with unconditional love. Sarah recalled how, when she was eight or nine years old, she cut her hair. "When I showed my mother, she seemed disappointed." A few days later, when her mother left home to go on a long trip, Sarah thought her mother had left because she was upset about her haircut. Feeling dismissed and rejected, she sought comfort in overeating. "That's when food first became my friend," Sarah recounted.

Believing that my parents' love was conditional, and that it could be spontaneously withdrawn based on the slightest infringement, whether real or perceived, was something I had experienced as a child as well, I told her. "For me, though, food was not my friend; it was my enemy," I continued. "My father actually used food as a method of control; always prepared, served, and consumed just the way, and only the way, he liked it: unseasoned and tasteless. And I was expected to eat it the same way, every last bit of it."

Rebelling, I refused to eat most of the food I was given, crying incessantly at the dining room table until, out of frustration and anger, my father would ultimately allow me to leave, shouting, "I don't care if you eat or not!" Yet even though his yelling caused more tears, I was relieved to finally walk away from that dining room table and his authoritarian control.

I also told Sarah how, in contrast to being condemned for being overweight, I was chastised for being underweight. Barely tipping the scale at one hundred pounds when I graduated from high school at sixteen, I was incessantly ridiculed by family, friends, and even teachers, both openly and publicly. "You got a seventy-eight, the same as your weight," my high school French teacher announced in front of the entire class while holding up my test paper's results. I felt humiliated, consumed with shame.

Sarah's eyes became softer and more compassionate as she listened to my story, reflecting the shared feelings of shame we both felt for being unfairly criticized for our appearance. As women who not only experienced, but also touted, the personal benefits of learning from others, we fell into an easy conversation about our lives.

"How did you overcome your feelings of insecurity?" she asked me. I told her that I underwent many years of psychotherapy, beginning at age twenty-four and, as a result, even returned to school to become a psychologist myself, so I could help others who suffered from similar childhood experiences. Just as Sarah undertook a role as a national spokesperson to help others address and take control of their health challenges, I had wanted to do the same.

In the Fall 2004 edition of *Work Life Matters*, which featured NYU Medical Center as its cover story, Sarah Ferguson's personal story of internal courage served as its crowning glory. Entitled "Turquoise Stockings," this feature article not only paid homage to her sincerity, empathy, and bravery, but to her audacity in ignoring her critics by finding courage solely and completely within herself.

AMY FERRIS

"No more crumbs."

—AMY FERRIS, Writer. Author. Speaker.
Warrior. Goddess. Badass.
(Facebook profile self-description)

I met Amy Ferris in the Summer of 2017 at an event and panel discussion hosted by Take The Lead Women, an organization whose mission is to establish gender parity in US leadership by 2025. The room was filled with feminists, some wearing name badges, others not. I didn't recognize anyone when I first walked in, but then I saw a familiar face.

"Has anyone ever told you that you look like Meryl Streep?" I asked a woman as she walked by. I looked down at her name tag: Amy Ferris. It was familiar to me, but I wasn't sure why. I soon discovered that she had been an original board member of the Women's Media Center, an organization founded by Gloria Steinem, Jane Fonda, and Robin Morgan. This led us to a further conversation about Gloria. I told Amy I'd written an article about

Gloria for the *Huffington Post* in celebration of her eightieth birthday a few years earlier.

"You wrote that?" Amy replied, with a surprised look on her face. "I printed out that article. I loved it. It was so real."

Having become a friend of Amy's over the past two years, I look back on that encounter and realize how important that word—"real"—is to Amy. Being real is something Amy not only admires in others but exudes herself. She is always present, her eyes focused solely and entirely on whomever she is speaking with. This is especially true when she's with women, and particularly with women whom she sees as needing to embrace their true worth. "No more crumbs," she is known for often saying and writing in her Facebook posts. "You deserve the whole shebang!"

Amy is an author, writer, editor, activist, screenwriter, playwright, high-school dropout, and self-described ruckus maker. Her memoir, *Marrying George Clooney, Confessions from a Midlife Crisis,* was adapted into an off-Broadway play in 2012. Her screenplay, *Funny Valentines,* was nominated for a Best Screenplay award (STARZ/BET) in 2000. She also cowrote the film, *Mr. Wonderful,* and has edited two anthologies, *Dancing at The Shame Prom* (2012) and *Shades of Blue* (2015).

Amy often writes about what and whom she loves, as she did on *marryinggeorgeclooney.com,* the web site dedicated to her memoir: "I love writing about (all things) women. I love championing and supporting and encouraging and inspiring women, and my fervent wish (and prayer) is that all women awaken to their greatness: using their lives fully, with passion, compassion, determination, hope, self-fullness, humor, truth, authenticity, power, boldness, kindness, and forgiveness. I want women to forgive themselves for all those old antiquated belief systems that were instilled and engraved in their lives by others who just didn't know any better."

Amy invited me to interview her for this book in August 2019 at one of her favorite spots, the Hotel Fauchere in Milford,

Pennsylvania, the town where she resides. Built in 1852, the building is not only historic but authentic, remaining true to the Relais & Chateaux "5C" motto—character, courtesy, calm, charm, and cuisine. The large brick and white gothic Italian-style building stands on the corner of West Catherine Street, a street filled with quaint and eclectic restaurants, antique shops, and mom-and-pop retail stores.

When I arrive, Amy is seated at a table on the outside deck, just in front of the beautiful, glass-enclosed dining room. It's a bright and sunny day. Amy greets me in her signature style, by cupping my face in her hands as she places a kiss on my lips. We each order a glass of white wine (her favorite) and salad.

Before we get into the interview, I excuse myself to use the restroom, which is located inside the hotel at the bottom of a mahogany wood staircase. The walls on both sides of the stairs are adorned with signed headshots of honored hotel guests, including former US Presidents Theodore Roosevelt, John F. Kennedy, and Bill Clinton; celebrities like Babe Ruth, Mae West, and Rudolph Valentino; and famous writers like Alistair Cooke, Robert Frost—and Amy Ferris. Her framed headshot hangs between famed film directors Lionel Barrymore and Cecil B. DeMille. While Amy Ferris may not be a household name, to all those who have come to know her, her spot among these luminaries has been well-earned.

As I join Amy upstairs at our outdoor table, I ask her when she is planning to host another writing workshop in New York City. I first came to learn about her workshop, "Women Writing/ Righting Their Lives," on Facebook (or "Gracebook," as she calls it) soon after we first met. She describes it this way online: "The most extraordinary things happen when women get together— when we write/share our stories, write/right our lives—we give each other the courage and inspiration and absolute permission to be huge and audacious, fierce and mighty—to be fucking Goddess/Warriors. Bring your computer, a pen, some paper, and a pad," it continued. "A story you wanna share, a truth you wanna spill, a secret that you've tucked, locked away that needs to be released and sent on its way. This is a safe, sacred space where we get to change our lives."

I signed up for the workshop even before I read the description in its entirety. And, yes, it did change my life.

Three days before the workshop, Amy sent us three writing prompts: 1) Broken Open, 2) Assisted Loving, and 3) I Pick Me. We could choose one, two, or all three to write about, but they must be read aloud, she warned. "This is how we dig deep. You will not be critiqued or judged, and this workshop is not about craft. It's about changing our lives, declaring our worth, owning our greatness, standing in our power. This is how we become women of unlimited self-esteem."

At the start of the workshop, I read this aloud to the group of twelve:

I pick me.
I pick me because no one else can.
I've tried. It just never worked.
Looking back, I have always found that I knew the
right thing to do.
And to not do.
But I allowed myself to be persuaded, dissuaded,
due to doubt,
The doubt of others, as well as putting others' needs
before my own.
While moving all others to the front.
It was the only way I was appreciated.
It became, indeed my identity.
Until one day, that shelf fell, but it didn't break into
charred pieces.
I was there to catch it, to cradle it.
Finally, I caught myself.

Reading a personal piece aloud, publicly, is an experience like no other. There is a unique freedom and power we experience from the support and acceptance from a room full of strangers. Amy was right. I did feel empowered when I read aloud. As each of the twelve women in the room read their writing, a camaraderie formed, and a sense of community was developed. After the end of four hours of writing and reading, then more writing and reading to a number of different prompts, Amy asked us to do one more thing:

"Write a Dear John or Dear Jane letter to something or someone you no longer need or want in your life; something that has kept you small, invisible, not believing in your own greatness; someone or something that has caused you great pain."

Mine was a letter to my mother. After we each read our letters aloud, Amy asked us to hand all of them to her. "I will take them home and throw them into a fire," she said. "No more pain."

That was the first of four workshops I participated in over the next year and a half, and each time I felt more empowered, respected, and accepted by every one of the women who participated along with me. It therefore seemed logical to bring Amy's words, and love, to as many other women as possible.

In 2018, I invited her to write a regular column for Women's eNews, which she named "WRighteous." Announcing this new column in Women's eNews, I invited our readers into "Amy's world, to champion, encourage, and inspire women to awake to their greatness, as only she can, through passion, truth, hope, and humor—along with a heaping side of activism." She didn't waste any time getting to it. In her first column, introducing "WRighteous," she wrote, "I will stand up on a soapbox and remind you that we have unlimited power, untapped power, and that anger is not power. This is the place where I will remind you, as I constantly remind myself, that we have become the women our mothers longed to be, always wanted to be. This is the place where I will demand that we all—each of us—take down the walls that we have built around ourselves, the walls that keep us from being intimate, keep us from sharing our down and dirty, keep us from sharing our truth, keep us from exposing the very stories that move and rattle and shake and, yes, understand another human heart."

"WRighteous" was just the first of several collaborations between Women's eNews and Amy Ferris. The other, which Amy named "The Ovary Office," is a video series that reports on the true qualifications and accomplishments of each female candidate running for public office in 2020. "Rather than her electability or likability, which too often takes precedence in traditional coverage of female politicians," I wrote in the series' introduction, "Amy Ferris, with her usual fierceness, will write about each candidate's expertise, policies, and goals for the future of the US with accuracy, honesty, and transparency."

In her first article, "The Ovary Office: This Is No Time for Polite," Amy opens by writing: "Women have been told to sit down and keep quiet, to stand off to the side and stay out of view. Polite is a first cousin to nice; both are rooted in fear and worry, preventing us from standing tall, standing up, and standing for whom and what we believe in, allowing others to get ahead at our expense. Polite may give us the shirt off its back, but it will never allow us to stand on it, and it most certainly won't have ours. Polite will never have our back."

As we finished our lunch, Amy told me that someone had recently asked her where she learned to love other people the way she does. She told me about an experience she had as a child in response, which she also posted on her blog, "Post Coffee, Pre Wine," which is also now a podcast.

It went like this:

Where did you learn to love the way you love?

Here's a taste. The bag sat on my lap, and she told me to hold on to it tight.

"Don't let it spill open," she said, while she chain-smoked.

We pulled into a driveway, the car now in park.

A deep breath, a deep sigh, a deep exhale of cigarette smoke combined.

She took the bag off my lap, and I watched as she walked up the stoop and rang the doorbell, and then she disappeared into a split level.

A good forty-five-minute drive from where we lived out on Long Island.

I sat, fidgety, minding my own business and everything else from inside the car.

After what felt like forever in little girl years, she came out of the house cradling her purse. The man stood on the porch and waved to me. I waved back.

I had no idea who he was, but my mother always reminded me to be nice to her friends.

She placed her purse on the seat between us, and while I was concocting a million stories in my head about what happened to the bag that sat on my lap, she lit a cigarette, opened the window a crack, and then motioned for me to open her purse.

And there smack in the middle—as if it were standing at attention—was a ring.

A man's pinky ring. Two diamond chips on either side of a tiger eye stone set in platinum.

"Where's your jewelry, Mommy, where?"

"Well, I made a trade, I traded some of my jewelry for this, for Daddy's birthday. It's a surprise, a secret, so don't say anything. Cross your heart."

I crossed my heart.

". . . and hope to die?" I asked.

"No, no . . . it's enough to cross your heart," she replied.

We were broke, struggling, a bad set of circumstances spiraled, setting our lives back, and we were barely eking by. Barely.

She threw him a small dinner party at our house with some of their nearest and dearest, and after he blew out the candles and made a wish, she placed the little black box on the table, and when he opened it his eyes filled, and my mother leaned in and kissed him—long and hard—and in what seemed like a whisper—stuck, lodged in her throat—she wished him a happy birthday and many more, and then he slipped the ring on his pinky, and it felt as if he grew an inch or two taller as he stared at this gift, this unexpected gift filled with so much love.

A little over a year later, while our lives were still on hold, slowly but surely regaining some ground, it was my mom's birthday. He was taking her out to a favorite restaurant of hers, and even though it would cost him an arm and a leg, he was willing to give up those body parts for her. A giant, gift-wrapped box sat on the dining room table, a card leaning up against it; her name, Bea, written in his impeccable gorgeous handwriting on the envelope. She was dressed to the nines, her hair coiffed, her face made up. Her lipstick matched her dress, magenta. "Mommy, open it open it open it," I had no idea what it was, but I loved gift-wrapped presents. They were filled with hope. My father stood next to the table as she unwrapped the box—a brand-new leather jewelry box, three drawers thick. She looked up at him, and he nodded and gestured for her to open it. There in the jewelry box were the pieces she had pawned to buy him the ring—her jewelry polished and shiny and ready to wear.

Years later my Dad told me the story. "A little O'Henry-ish," I said.

"Yes," he said, smiling. "Yes." The jeweler, the nice man I waved to, was a good friend of my dad's. He owned a jewelry store on West 47th Street—the jewelry district—and he held on to my mom's jewelry, knowing he would give it back to my dad.

"What do I owe you," my dad asked his friend.

"The pleasure of your friendship," he said.

They remained good friends until my dad died.

My dad's pinky ring, along with a few of my mom's pieces, live side-by-side in a jewelry box that Ken [Amy's husband] gave me.

All this to say: Please, believe in love and goodness and hope.

And she does, along with everyone who has the good fortune to come to know her.

photo © Michael Angelo

LEYMAH GBOWEE

*"Violence was never an option. We were prepared to even
have our bodies walked on if it would bring about peace."*

—Leymah Gbowee, 2011 Nobel Peace Prize recipient

"My work has taken me to many places, and I have never been
to a place or a country on this earth where my curious
eyes—and trust me, I look around—have not seen a situation
in need of change, even in this great America, from homeless
people, to teen mothers, to drug addicts, to corrupt political leaders, to military dictatorships," said Leymah Gbowee, the 2011
Nobel Peace Prize winner who organized protests that helped
end a bloody civil war in Liberia, during our interview in 2012.
"All of these things, in these communities, make life very gray.
For many individuals, a smile is difficult to come by. Hope is
lacking in their vocabulary. Like Liberians a few years ago, many
of those living in these places thought life has no true meaning."

But Leymah Gbowee learned from historic male peacemakers, like Dr. Martin Luther King and Mahatma Gandhi, about
how to effectively use nonviolence as a weapon to create change.
An even stronger influence for the Liberian Mass Action for

Peace were female characters from the sacred texts who did great things, such as Esther, Deborah, and Rehab, the prostitute in the Bible, and Khadijah, the wife of the prophet Mohammad. "These women were the archetypes that inspired what the women of Liberia did to bring peace to their country, rather than an awareness of nonviolent political action in other countries," Leymah said to me. "There was never a point during the Liberian uprising when us women considered using violence."

This is just a sampling of the inspirational words and thoughts Leymah Gbowee expressed as Vassar College's commencement speaker in 2012. It was the same year that my son was graduating from Vassar, and I was thrilled to hear that she was granting only one interview—and that was to me. I would get to interview her the day before the graduation ceremony in one of Vassar's classrooms. I was then a contributor to *The Huffington Post*, and since my son was in the 2012 graduating class, she felt I was the best choice. While I considered myself fortunate, I was unaware of just how memorable this experience would be until I actually sat down with her.

When she arrived, she was dressed in her country's traditional West African attire: a long and brightly colored wrap skirt, called a *lappa*, and a loose-fitting blouse called a *bubba*. Since Liberia lies fewer than five hundred miles from the equator, breathable clothing is necessary to keep cool. She also wore a head wrap, weaving a brightly colored pattern of pink, yellow, and blue.

The name Liberia comes from the English word "liberty," which is particularly ironic since the country's politics had been dominated by armed men since 1980. Further, Charles Taylor, Liberia's twenty-second President, was charged with war crimes as a result of his involvement in the Sierra Leone Civil War (1991–2002), when he illegally militarized children as young as nine years old. Since children were often the first to be sent out to the front lines, thousands were killed, while many others became victims of torture, abduction, and forced labor. Unsurprisingly, many of the militarized girls experienced the worst abuse by also being raped and sexually enslaved. The United Nations estimates that approximately 15,000 children were illegally militarized.

Leymah Gbowee, herself, was one person who enabled Liberia to live up to its name, and she did it through peace. Launching the women's nonviolent peace movement, Women of Liberia Mass Action for Peace, to help bring an end to the war, she and the women she mobilized released a campaign that called for nonviolence and peace. As its leader, Leymah wanted to take Liberia's future into her own hands by saying no to violence and yes to peace. After forcing a meeting with President Charles Taylor where he agreed to attend upcoming peace talks in Ghana, the Liberian women also traveled to Ghana and surrounded the room. Dressed all in white, the women threatened to remove all of their clothes, which would have been considered a cultural dishonor. One of the reasons Leymah took this dramatic step was that the peace talks had gone on for months, after initially being scheduled to take only two weeks, and the fighting in Liberia was continuing to escalate. Further, just that morning, the American embassy in Liberia had been bombed, which fueled the women's desperation to change the dynamic at the peace talks in Ghana. They also blocked all the doors and windows, preventing the men from escaping, until a peaceful resolution to ending the war was instituted.

Ultimately, these efforts resulted in a free election in 2005 that Leymah's collaborator, Ellen Johnson Sirleaf, won, and they were both awarded the 2011 Nobel Peace Prize "for their nonviolent struggle for the safety of women and for women's rights to full participation in peace-building work."

For a woman who has exhibited such strength and bravery, Leymah, who describes herself as "a warrior without a weapon," spoke to me in a strong yet gentle voice. She recalled those desperate days during the Civil War where "the opposition did not know how to embrace our brokenness. We weren't living at that time; we were only surviving. We were glad to wake up in the morning but scared to be alive, happy to see night fall but afraid to fall asleep." Then, she spoke about the importance of moving beyond thinking only about one's own personal comfort, instead placing a priority on the health and safety of others. "I recall the many days when I and my fellow protesters went without water, often in ninety-degree heat," she said. "But when you get to a place where death is better than life, you have nothing to lose."

She also warned of people's tendency to believe that they will always be protected from the violence that afflicts others. "Let me tell you something," she continued. "If you think there are social problems and you are comfortable inside your fence, trust me, if you don't help to address those problems, they'll come knocking at your door. We were concerned about one thing—securing a future for Liberia by creating a safe space for our children to grow up and be what we, the parents, could not be for many reasons." So with no budget, no international backing, and no previous experience as activists, they stepped out to change their children's lives by repeatedly shouting from the streets, "Peace for Liberia Now!"

And these four words not only became their nonviolent "battle cry," but the armor that ultimately shrouded them in safety. In fact, it was their refusal to bear arms that proved the most disarming to their oppressors.

Leymah Gbowee relayed all of this to me in what turned out to be the perfect setting. Founded in 1861, Vassar has a history of bravery and independence as well, defying patriarchal-imposed restrictions while maintaining its identity and true purpose. Only the second degree-granting institution of higher education for women in the United States, the college was created to provide an education equal to Harvard and Yale, considered the best men's colleges at that time. One of Vassar College's crowning glories, in fact, is The Great Window, a massive stained-glass window measuring sixty-seven feet long by twenty-four feet wide in the Thompson Memorial Library, which represents one of the most memorable events in women's higher education. It depicts the conferring of the first Doctorate of Philosophy degree to a woman, Lady Elena Lucretia Cornaro-Piscopia (in 1678) by the University of Padua, who was previously denied the examination for the doctor of theology degree.

The importance of women's education isn't lost on Leymah. Considering it to be a primary vehicle for the future of Liberia's children, she told me that she is "continually reminded about the promise of education in creating bright futures for our children." She then relayed an experience that had occurred only a few days earlier. "While in Thailand for the Rotary International 106th Convention, I was being driven to the convention center, and the young lady who was responsible for protocol asked me, 'Leymah, how do you as a young woman respond to bosses who have a problem with smartness?' I told her, 'Keep being smart. Don't apologize to anyone for your intelligence.'"

In tribute to Leymah's work, Vassar College, in partnership with Leymah's foundation, the Gbowee Peace Foundation, granted full scholarships to two West African women entering as freshman in 2012, which would not only help them earn their college degrees, but would cover all expenses necessary for these students to study at Vassar for four years. "Scholarship unlocks intelligence," Leymah said. "And not nearly enough women in West Africa have support to follow their dreams." She is particularly pleased that Vassar is providing full four-year scholarships to two women rather than the more common one-year scholarships offered to more women by some other colleges, often leaving these students without the funding to complete their degree. "I believe in quality over quantity, since the girls who graduate can then provide a strong symbol of hope for other girls that they can achieve too," she said. "This, I feel, provides the strongest impact."

Still, while Leymah's positive outlook of hope for those who have been impacted the most by violence has enabled her to make such a difference in the lives of others, her humility does not allow her to take full credit. "If you look very closely in the poorest of communities, you will see everyday heroes and 'sheroes.' They are the ones who are symbols of hope. They are the only ones who can extract a smile from a mother who has no idea where she will get money for medication and money for food," she said. "These are men and women who have committed their lives to bringing relief to those in pain. Some are doctors, bankers, corporate managers, community workers, or peace activists; these are men and women who know where they have been planted, and their purpose is to blossom."

As such, during her commencement speech to the graduating Class of 2012, she urged them to follow their callings. "It is a known fact that people who feel a sense of calling in a particular field will bring more enthusiasm to their work than those who are performing nine-to-five, get-on-with-it, make my money and go home jobs," she said. "There are clear distinctions in the way they perform their duties. The ones who feel a sense of calling blossom, while the ones who feel it's nine-to-five work make money. In most instances, they leave trails of dead leaves."

She further spoke about her own determination that stopped the violence in her country, and of the sacrifices made by many other ordinary women, in her speech. "No one took a salary, no one was coerced, and everyone came to the action willingly, knowing that they had been planted at that point to make change. Many of the women abandoned their businesses to be involved. Protesting was a way of life for many months."

She ended her speech by telling the graduates, "It is my hope and prayer that the dreams of changing the world that many of you had in your head when you left high school and entered college will still be the driving force and passion as you deliver services in whatever field you have been called to impact."

And when I asked her, just before the ending of our interview, what she had done to celebrate her own honor as a Nobel

Peace Prize winner, she said she had not done so yet, choosing instead to view this time as one of reflection. "I want to be able to look back on this honor and see women who are now standing on their own because of me," she told me. "Now that I got it, I have to earn it!"

photo © Howard Schatz

BILLIE JEAN KING

"Great leaders shine a light on others."
—BILLIE JEAN KING, thirty-nine-time
Grand Slam winning tennis player

"When I was thirteen years old and had been playing tennis tournaments for just over a year, I looked around and wondered why everyone wore white clothes, white shoes, and everyone who played was white. I remember asking myself, 'Where is everyone else?' Billie Jean King said during my interview with her in 2014. "But to believe you can also be a leader, it is important to see someone already in that position, someone who has already broken through barriers to set an example. Essentially, you have to see it to be it."

I met Billie Jean King for the first time at New York City's Plaza Hotel, where she was being honored as an "Outstanding Woman Leader" by the Women's Forum of New York. Every November, this women-only organization provides educational funding for women who are thirty-five and over, and whose educations were previously disrupted by extreme adversity. King's career of facing and overcoming adversity, both on and off the court, seemed particularly apropos for a recipient of this award. As she was standing backstage, waiting to be announced, I was introduced to her as a contributor for *The Huffington Post* who was interested in writing a profile about her. She was dressed in a royal-blue blazer and black pants, and her eyes beamed through the round, red-rimmed glasses that had become a long-standing staple of her attire. While shaking hands, I briefly told her how important her long-term commitment to gender equality in sports was to me, particularly as a teenager in the seventies, when she had not only challenged, but also triumphed over numerous barriers to gender equality. Since there was not enough time to conduct an interview, however, King looked to her communications manager, standing just a few feet away, and asked him to invite me to a symposium King was hosting the following week. "We weren't planning to invite any press," she said to me, "but I'd like you to be there."

The day-long symposium took place at New York's Museum of Natural History, where King announced the launch of her initiative, the Billie Jean King Leadership Institute (BJKLI). Its goals were twofold: to understand the challenges to achieving true diversity and inclusion in the workplace, and to develop the economic and commercial rationales for instituting, and sustaining, diversity and inclusion in the workforce and establishing equal pay for equal work in the marketplace.

It was not surprising that King, then seventy, was furthering her commitment to expanding and encouraging equality off the tennis court, after having done so much on the court throughout her twenty-five-year career. It seemed like only yesterday, in 1973, when I, along with over ninety million others, watched her play one singular and groundbreaking tennis match against Bobby Riggs. Dubbed the "Battle of the Sexes," it was that and much, much more. Riggs was a former top men's player, then a fifty-five-year-old self-described male chauvinist, who claimed that women tennis players were so inferior to male tennis players that even someone as old as he was could beat a top female player. More than just wanting to defeat Riggs on the court, King felt incredible pressure to win because, as she said to the press afterward, "I thought it would set us back fifty years if I didn't win that match. It would ruin the women's [tennis] tour, could weaken Title IX, and could impact the women's movement and affect all women's self-esteem. At twenty-nine years old, beating a fifty-five-year-old guy was no thrill for me. The thrill was exposing a lot of new people to tennis and changing the hearts and minds of people to more closely align with my lifelong goal of equality for all."

King did win, with relative ease, in three straight sets. I recall my feelings of relief, and inspiration, as I watched King raise her tennis racket in victory. At that moment, she proved that gender does not define us, nor limit us. Yet her victory that day was only the beginning of what she would accomplish for women on the court. One year earlier, King had threatened to boycott the US Open if equal prize money was not awarded to women and men. And while she also won that challenge, she told me, "It still took another thirty-four years before Wimbledon and the three other major tournaments decided to do the same for women [in 2007]. And still, today, women tennis players do not receive equal prizes at all tournaments." That same year, she also founded the Women's Tennis Association to create a better future for women's tennis and, one year later, founded the Women's Sports Foundation, dedicated to creating leaders by ensuring all girls access to sports.

Beyond the sport of tennis, King hopes to show through her Leadership Initiative how, due to unconscious bias, there is still a tremendous amount of untapped human potential in the working world. "We need leaders—in both the public and private sectors—to look at differences in the workplace through a lens where individuals are embraced for their unique contributions rather than judged, discounted, or alienated for what makes them different," King said at the beginning of her speech to a room full of attendees at New York's Museum of Natural History. "Just as I wouldn't want everyone on my team to just have a great backhand, we need a lot of different skills to win."

Yet struggles for equality do not exist solely around gender, and King is no stranger to another kind of struggle against discrimination. In fact, it is something we both share. We discussed this during our second interview two years later in 2017, at another of her Leadership Initiative's symposiums, which was held at The Paley Center for Media in New York City, a cultural institution dedicated to the discussion of the cultural, creative, and social significance in television and film.

It took place just before the film, *Battle of the Sexes*, was released. A biographical sports film based on the 1973 tennis match, its storyline also focused on King's closeted homosexuality, something she said she didn't feel comfortable with until she was in her fifties, even though she had been "outed" years earlier by a woman who filed a lawsuit contending that she was entitled to share in King's assets because of their lesbian relationship. "Being gay was a big deal in the seventies," King recalls, "and I was concerned that it would have a negative impact on women's professional tennis."

In reply, I told King, "It wasn't until I reached the age of forty-nine that I came out."

Surprised yet heartened by my response, King turned the spotlight on me. Eager to learn about my personal struggles and how I overcame them, she said, humbly, "I learn so much from others, and everyone has something to share."

I relayed to her how I felt during my early teen years, being attracted to girls but terrified to admit it, even to myself. Mocked by my family and friends for participating in competitive sports, I couldn't bear any further subjugation. My mother, in particular, refused to watch me participate in any sports until one day, after I pleaded with her to come to the softball field to watch me play, she finally did. I sat in the dugout, awaiting my turn at bat. I was pleasantly surprised to see her arrive, and I watched her intently from the opposite side of the field as she walked toward the benches just beyond the right field fence. I thought, *What if I don't get a hit or, worse, strike out?* I desperately wanted to avoid disappointing her, but, after no more than five or ten minutes, she left before I even had a chance to step up to the plate.

"It wasn't until thirty-five years later," I told King, "that I acknowledged my true orientation." After two marriages, two divorces, and two children, I finally felt free to date women, but only after I eliminated one very influential person from my life: my mother. Always terrified to upset her, disappoint her, or worse, lose her, I kept my true self secret, until one day when I finally put myself first.

"If people can't live authentically at home or at work, not only will they suffer, but everything else around them will as well," King told me after I finished my story.

And that is exactly what King is determined to change. Since there is no US federal law that adequately protects lesbian, gay, bisexual, and transgender (LGBT) workers from employment discrimination, many of us are afraid to reveal our true selves at work. Further, in twenty-eight states, there are no explicit statewide laws at all protecting people from discrimination on the basis of sexual orientation or gender identity in employment, housing, and public accommodations. Additionally, more than four in ten lesbian, gay, and bisexual people have experienced some form of employment discrimination at some point in their lives, based on their sexual orientation, and ninety percent of transgender employees have experienced harassment, mistreatment, or discrimination on the job.

"So where does the long-term answer to ending all forms of discrimination lie?" I asked King.

"It's up to the millennials and future generations," she replied, at the end of our interview. "They are now having the greatest impact on diversity, equality, and inclusion, since millennials' views of diversity and inclusion at their organizations are quite different from those of baby boomers and Gen Xers. They are getting their organizations to think differently about how to attract talent, interact at work, and redefine inclusion." King straightened her red-rimmed glasses, while leaning forward to accentuate this last point. "The alternative, where everybody thinks alike, is unacceptable. Every person in the US is an immigrant, and we need those different perspectives. That is how we find solutions." She then looked off in the distance, reminiscing about the platform that got her here. "We must champion each other and bring out the best in us."

As we said our good-byes, our opening handshake turned into a hug. And as the iconic sports giant walked back to the symposium with one of her staff, it was her compassion and humility that lingered long after.

GLORIA STEINEM

"Vote!"

—Gloria Steinem, author and activist

"It's outrageous that so many citizens didn't vote in the 2016 election," said Gloria Steinem, the human rights activist and iconic leader of the American feminist movement. "If voter turnout had been the same as it was when Obama first ran for president, Trump would have lost. But the good news is," she continued, "that his presidency has activated more people, particularly women, than I've ever seen in my lifetime, more than even during the Vietnam War."

It was now just two months before the November 2018 midterm elections, which would see the Democratic party win back the House of Representatives. Women's eNews had been increasingly reporting on the surge of women candidates running for Congress, as well as their ideas, policies, and proposals to protect women's rights while promoting gender equality. We'd recently launched a new weekly series entitled, "Us in the US," to alert our national and international readers to the Trump Administration's growing anti-women sentiment and legislation, in hopes of urging those in political office to take a stronger stance to support women's rights before they are further curtailed. After a few articles in the series were published, I was unsure of its impact. I therefore contacted Gloria in hopes of meeting with her to get her advice. She responded within twenty-four hours, and a meeting was scheduled for just a few weeks later.

While receiving a response from Gloria Steinem in less than a day may seem surprising to most, it was not at all to me. Having met her for the first time twenty-five years earlier during her book tour for *Revolution from Within* (published in 1992), I recall drumming up just enough courage to mention that I was also a writer (although not yet published), as I timidly handed her my book to sign. Rather than just signing her name, she personalized it with the following message: "To a Sister Writer." This was all I needed to cement my future as a feminist writer. In the years that followed, as I became a published writer, launched my own feminist magazine (*Work Life Matters*), and then became executive director of Women's eNews (a global women's news organization), I have come to expect no less from Gloria, no matter the time or location. When I wrote an article for the *Huffington Post* in tribute to her turning eighty years old (in 2014), she responded within twenty-four hours with an email personally thanking me, while she was traveling through India riding elephants, humanely of course. When I wrote an article about coming out as gay in the *Huffington Post* in 2016, she immediately sent me an email expressing her support for my bravery, as well as her sorrow for my having needed to live, at any time, untrue to myself. And in 2018, when I published a link in Women's eNews to my speaking publicly, for the very first time, about being sexually abused by my brother, my mother's refusal to acknowledge it, and why I now sleep in a T-shirt courageously sporting the boldly written message, "Be the Woman You Always Needed As a Girl," she wrote to me the following day:

Dearest Lori–
Your letter about your abuse by your brother—and
your mother's lack of response—is moving and cou-
rageous—and actually an opening into a kind of abuse
also suffered by two friends of mine, too, yet rarely
included in studies of abuse. Thank you thank you!
And I love that T-shirt!
and you!
Gloria

The day of our meeting, Gloria welcomed me into her New York City apartment with a warm and all-embracing hug. She was dressed in black, her hair tied back in a small ponytail. Her tall, thin figure appeared gentle, yet self-assured. In her presence, I always feel completely at home, since we have, over the years, had prearranged meetings like this one, been photographed together on red carpets at various galas, and spontaneously run into each other at numerous feminist events in New York City, which we both call home. Her two-story apartment displays the historical splendor of a life fully lived. On every wall hangs a multitude of paintings and photographs reflecting the diversity of human rights activists who have come before and after her. No space is left untouched, playing host to a unique display of furniture, sculpture, and crafts collected from over six decades of global travel. "This apartment is the best thing that ever happened to me," said Gloria, who moved in over fifty years ago, when the rent was only three hundred dollars a month for one floor. "It was much cheaper to first rent and then buy an apartment." She ultimately bought the apartment a few years later for a mere $27,000.

Standing against a wall at the entrance to her office is a replica of a New York City street sign stamped boldly with the words, MS. MAGAZINE WAY, a newly named street on the corner of East 32nd Street and Third Avenue in Manhattan, standing in tribute to the iconic magazine that had once been located at

207 East 32nd St. "At first, I thought this was the only free block they had left," Gloria chuckled, her humor and humility always present. She then introduced me to her new cat, Aphendum. "This cat only has three paws, which she is completely unaware of. My niece, who is a rescuer of cats, decided I should have a three-legged cat," she said with a wide grin.

As we sat down to talk, I first asked Gloria her thoughts about how Women's eNews can best utilize its resources as a global, nonprofit news outlet to ensure women's rights do not decline even further under the current presidential administration. Gloria responded by speaking of the critical importance of getting people out to vote during the midterm elections. "We need to gather people on the ground to get as many people to vote as possible," she said, "and the best way to do so is through bitable bites." By the end of our discussion the new weekly series, "3 for V," was born, where Women's eNews invites its readers to ask three people per day (at home, at work, at the gym, etc.) these three questions: 1. Are you registered to vote? 2. Do you know where to vote? and 3. Do you know who your state legislators are? "It's doing things like these on a regular basis that are directed toward the levers of power that actually work." Gloria added.

This was not the first time I had sought out Gloria's advice. It actually started long before I met her; so long ago, in fact, that I was still living under my parents' roof. While I did not personally know her then, her speeches, essays, and books provided me with the hope and positivity I so desperately needed to counterbalance my toxic childhood.

I'd grown up hearing one prevailing word from my parents: *wrong*. As far back as I can remember, my parents consistently, and emphatically, told me I was *wrong*! Sometimes this word was hurled at me via a rhetorical question, "What's *wrong* with you?" Other times, it was more declarative and decisive in nature, "There is something *wrong* with you!"

Eventually, I learned that what was "wrong" was my inability to fit neatly into the box they had built for me, one that was encased in traditional gender behaviors and values on all four sides. Excelling in competitive sports and academics (particularly math and science) was "highly inappropriate for a girl," they warned, particularly when my older brother did not.

It was not until I turned twelve years old that I discovered an alternate belief system, and it arrived in a monthly package measuring 8 ½ x 11 inches. *Ms.* magazine, the first national feminist publication to introduce the women's rights movement into the mainstream, provided an open window with an expansive view of what was possible for me, and females of all ages, who did not ascribe to patriarchal-imposed gender roles. Through its articles exploring such empowering themes as women's financial and emotional independence, education and career opportunities, and what gender equality could and would look like, I, for the very first time, learned that I wasn't completely alone in the world. It was particularly through its monthly "Letters to the Editor" section, espousing and exposing others' dissatisfaction with the traditional status quo from real women with real names from such far-off places like Jean from Prince Edward Island, Mary from Liking, Missouri, and Sally from Contoocook, New Hampshire, where I finally found my true home. Still, too many women opted for "Name withheld" below their published letters, hiding their secret wish for gender equality from those who knew them. I knew early on that I would dedicate my life's work to this cause. I imagined I could help women and girls feel less fearful, intimidated, and alone. To offer a beacon of hope in the darkness, which was what *Ms.* did for me.

After I graduated from college, however, my parents had different ideas for my future. Feeling imprisoned under their roof with no financial means to leave, I was pressured to become a secretary, via their veiled justification that by learning to type, I would have "something to fall back on." For me, failure was not an option, but my parents made it clear that if I didn't do exactly as they said, I would face daily pressure, criticism, and other forms of emotional abuse. Yet, I was not to be just any secretary, my father warned, but a secretary for the post office, where he spent his thirty-plus-year career. Not only would I ultimately retire thirty-five years later with lifetime medical benefits and a pension, as he had, but, my mother added excitedly, "You will work for an executive, in an office, with carpeting on the floor." Eventually, we reached an agreement. I would work as a secretary, but in the industry I preferred, magazine publishing. They ultimately agreed, particularly since these offices were mostly carpeted. I then spent two very long years doing so, barely getting by, and thankful for, once again, the help of *Ms. Magazine*. One letter to the editor, in particular, provided a very small, but life-saving, daily exercise to get me through:

> *"Ms. readers who are secretaries may be interested in my daily assertiveness practice, which never fails to give me a boost. I type my initials in upper case next to the upper-case initials of those of the originator's at the bottom of whatever correspondence it might be. Small, but daily."*
>
> —KAY KAVANAUGH, Oak Park, Illinois. April 1982

This would be my first and last secretarial job. I was determined to write about gender issues for any community or local newspaper that would publish my articles. Eventually my articles began to be published in major market newspapers and magazines, and then I launched my own magazine publishing firm in 2002, which celebrated the successes of women in male-dominated industries. This ultimately led to my current role as the executive director of Women's eNews, a nonprofit digital news organization covering the most crucial issues impacting women and girls around the world.

Since joining Women's eNews, I have purposely published more real-life stories from women and girls located in some of the most dangerous locations for females, who can uniquely describe their personal experiences. Clearly, attaching names and faces to articles, rather than just speaking in terms of quantities and totals, makes them more memorable and impactful.

I learned this in 2007, when Hillary Clinton and Barack Obama were campaigning for the Democratic presidential nomination. Gloria invited me to join a small group of women to share our writing, and we met every three weeks over six months. She was working on, among other things, her memoir (published in 2018); I was writing freelance op-eds for the *Huffington Post* and other mass-market publications; and the other members were working on everything from short stories to essays to books of their own.

Sitting in a small circle with these other women, around the living room table where *Ms.* magazine was born, I felt complete support and unconditional acceptance for the first time in my life. *There is nothing I could read or say or do that would be judged,* I thought. How freeing; how liberating. This gave me the courage to read a spontaneously written piece about an experience I had hidden, out of shame, for over forty years. It was the worst beating I'd ever experienced, condoned by my entire family. I was seven years old at the time. My brother and I had slept overnight at my maternal grandmother's house, as we would do from time to time to allow my parents a night out alone. My grandmother didn't like me, often threatening to "wash my mouth out with soap." I was too outspoken and independent for my age and gender, she repeatedly warned. After months of threatening to tell my father how I "misbehaved," one day she actually did. When my parents walked through the front door after their date, she barely had enough time to get all the words out about my misbehavior when my father rushed over to me, picked me up by my clothes, and threw me onto the floor, face down. My grandmother yelled "Again!" and he did. Each time I landed on the floor, my brother laughed. Finally, after hitting the floor five or six times, my mother yelled, "Enough!" After one or two more throws, he finally stopped. It was never discussed; no apologies were ever uttered.

When I read this experience aloud during one of our writing group sessions, I was greeted with unconditional compassion, empathy, and support. No, there was nothing I could say or do that would make me feel unwelcome and certainly not "wrong." The freedom to express this painful experience finally freed me from the shame and guilt I had shouldered for over four decades.

And this time, almost ten years later, those same feelings of unconditional support consumed me as I sat with Gloria in the first floor of her apartment, where her office resides. As I gave one last look around the room before leaving our meeting, I took note of the custom-built loft rising above the living room, draped in sheer white curtains sweeping across to the massive windows below. "I had this loft built for feminists to stay when they are visiting New York City," Gloria said. "In fact, I am leaving this entire apartment in my will to future feminists who need a home while traveling here." In response, I must have let out a short gasp or sigh at the very thought of Gloria leaving this world, my world. "Although," she quickly added, perhaps after picking up on my reaction, "I do plan to live to one hundred, since I have too many deadlines to meet."

Twenty-five who amplified this book:

TAINA BIEN-AIMÉ

"Women have always saved the world by fighting against evil, and by saving families and communities. If we didn't, the world would have become extinct a long, long time ago."

—TAINA BIEN-AIMÉ, executive director of the
Coalition Against Trafficking in Women

Her grandmother was a suffragist. Her mother was a rebel. And Taina grew up thinking women ran the world. "My world, anyway," she told me.

I first met Taina two years before our July 2019 interview when she was being honored for her commitment to end sex trafficking and the commercial sexual exploitation of women and girls through her organization, The Coalition Against Trafficking of Women.

What led her to this role was in some ways unique, yet in other ways not at all. From the beginning, it seemed, Taina was inspired by women inside her home as well as out. She described her childhood as a typical "daughter of immigrants' upbringing," since her mother emigrated from Haiti to the US at the age of eighteen. "My education about women came from the kitchen table," Taina recalled, "where men never entered, and where women who were strong family matriarchs, as well as those who were battered, cooked together, talked together, and came together." It was there that her mother often spoke about the importance of education for girls, and never to count on a man.

"One day, when I was in my teens, she gave me the first copy of *Ms.* magazine, and said, 'Pay attention to that white lady with the big glasses,' referring to Gloria Steinem." Yet, *Ms.* wasn't the only publication that influenced her early in life. "I read *Our Bodies, Ourselves* in one day, and Simone de Beauvoir's *The Second Sex* changed my life," she added. "It gave me the tools to understand the depth of women's inequality for the very first time."

We met up over coffee at a local New York City Upper West Side boutique hotel lobby, a place I like to call my "better office" due to its warm and inviting environment: wide-armed Victorian chairs, plush velvet couches basking in earth tone colors, and dimmed soft lighting, making my interviewees feel at ease. I'd found over many conversations with all kinds of women that this place encouraged engagement; here, consciousness could be unleashed.

Taina arrived dressed in all white, sporting a white summer dress with matching white leather loafers. She exudes a Kamala Harris look to me, seamlessly blending calm with assurance, her bright smile never wavering.

It was just one day after she'd appeared as a guest on two political talk shows, *Democracy Now* and *The Brian Lehrer Report*, to discuss the latest news revelations about sex trafficking crimes that were reaching the highest levels in the US government. Alexander Acosta, the Trump Administration's newest Labor Secretary, had just cut the international sex trafficking budget, while Jeffrey Epstein, a registered sex offender, financier, and long-time friend of Donald Trump, had been arrested one week earlier on charges of sex trafficking of a minor and conspiracy to engage in sex trafficking. Acosta had also just been exposed for arranging a plea deal in 2008 that kept Epstein, a convicted sex offender, out of prison. "This demonstrates the total failure of our country to protect women," Taina said.

It's failures like these that first inspired Taina to devote her life's work to helping women live in safety. "There was no other way for me to be but a warrior for women's lives," Taina reflected. Coming of age during the women's movement in the 1970s, when she was just in her early teens, she realized there was a whole world out there where women were subservient to their husbands. "But unlike my mother, who told me, 'If a man ever raises his hand at you, you better grab a frying pan and hit him on the head with it,' I chose a more socially acceptable way to protect women's rights, through peaceful activism and advocacy." She chuckled reflecting on her mother's unabashed candor, and then added, "I have always believed, in my heart of hearts, that even outside the kitchen, women are the most powerful beings on the planet, but how to get them to become the most powerful people in real life has always been the challenge."

Moving to Geneva, Switzerland, at age ten, she spent her next fourteen years being educated there. When she returned to New York City to work for an international organization, and as she was planning to apply to a PhD program in comparative literature, the dean recommended she go to law school. "Law school taught me that all institutions are created by men, and that in order to make systemic change, these structures need to change, which is what a lawyer can help do," she said. Seeing herself as one cog in the wheels of the social justice and human rights movements, she recounted, "Just as my foremothers worked hard but didn't live long enough to see the fruits of their struggles, knowing that their daughters and granddaughters would eventually benefit was enough for them, and it will be enough for me."

The timing of our interview was particularly fitting since it took place just two months after Taina penned an article for Women's eNews entitled, "Handmaids and Jezebels: New York Must Not Legalize Harm," reflecting her position on two crucial bills that would significantly impact women's rights. These bills, which Taina viewed as "defining women as vessels for economic profit," further concerned her since one of the bills was meant to legalize commercial reproductive surrogacy, thereby allowing anyone to rent women's wombs. The other would fully decriminalize the sex trade, including pimping, brothel owning, and sex buying. "These elected officials, under the guise of progressive politics, are saluting an acutely regressive status of women, jeopardizing their rights to health, safety, and bodily integrity, while also hindering any collective efforts to reach equality," she wrote in her commentary.

Yet, Taina is quick to assert that although The Coalition Against Trafficking of Women's work is primarily dedicated to the elimination of the sex trade, it would be dangerous for her, or any women's rights activists, to only work on one single issue. "Too often, we work in silos in the women's movement, because the amount of work to be done is so overwhelming," she cautioned. "But we can't slice up women's rights. We can't say that a woman has a right to vote but she cannot drive. We can't say that she has a right to bodily integrity but we're not going to address sexual exploitation in that same discussion." In fact, the entire question about what it means to be born female, and how governments and cultures generally view women as full human beings, forms the essence of her work. "Right now, we have a corporate culture where women are commodities. Underneath the beautiful package, which we are admired for, lies our dehumanization. The women's movement needs to remember that our rights are inalienable, universal, and indivisible."

For women of color, this is especially true. Drawing on the work of Toni Morrison, Taina reflected on the recently released documentary, *Toni Morrison: The Pieces I Am*. Paying tribute to

Morrison's lifelong work, the film unearths the history of black slavery, and black female slaves specifically. "The history of slavery has always been very male-centered," Taina contends. "Black women appear only as caricature. Her humanity and her suffering are never touched upon." Taina added, "What Ms. Morrison has gifted us is that the story of slavery is the story of black women." Similarly, Taina believes the unspoken stories by victims of sex trafficking need to be told to future generations, to prevent these victims, and their stories, from being lost forever. "We will never know the enormous contributions that could have been made had these women not been enslaved, battered, and murdered, because we don't even know the total number of women who have fallen victim to violence."

And even when stories are told, they can often be misrepresented. Case in point: Rosa Parks. "People think that Rosa Parks was just a tired, middle-aged woman, but she had decades of civil rights activism in her history," Taina pointed out. "Also, did you know that there is a picture of the seminal leaders from the civil rights movement in the White House—but only men are in it. If the photographer had only moved his camera a little to the left, it would have also included Dr. Dorothy Height, revered as the godmother of the civil rights movement. But her presence is lost in that photo."

What's not lost on Taina, however, is her hope for what she sees as a "rising generation." "I see young women in their twenties who already know that the essence of patriarchy is really about the control of women's reproductive systems." So what does a world of equality really look like for Taina? "Well, it's not about just focusing on the way women look, or the type of jobs we do." She specifically refers to Chairman Mao of China, who once commanded that women and men wear the same outfits, and work in the same trades. "Yet women were still raped and relegated to the most menial jobs."

In order to change this unyielding pattern of patriarchy that limits, and even eliminates, women's contributions to the world, she believes that "we need to work from the bottom up, and work on the ground with communities." Taina now sits forward in her chair, her eyes appearing more intent. "But we also need to partner with governments so that they change the laws to protect women's rights. This would be so easy for legislators to do, and then we could all just go home," she laments. Unfortunately, however, she believes that the issue of gender equality is not about resources, but about mentality. "Why are women so threatening to men?" she asks rhetorically.

And that's one critical reason she believes it's increasingly important to start having conversations with men, and with the men's groups that are working to end men's violence against women. In fact, Taina believes this is key to overturning the toxic way women are viewed in society. "They can say things that women can never say, like how they were raised to dominate women."

While Taina takes some comfort in the fact that women have come a long way, from achieving suffrage, to earning higher levels of education, to determining how many children they have, "This progress is very fragile," she cautioned. "We are always just one election away, or just one war away from women again becoming fodder for annihilation." She points to Iraq, Nigeria, the Congo, and even America today as examples. "If a woman has a miscarriage in some states now, she can actually go to prison," she says, shaking her head in disbelief.

Still, it's the next generation she believes in, and rests her hopes on, for the ultimate achievement of gender equality. Believing that a fourth feminist wave is "being formed right now," she closed our interview by reaffirming this point: "The resistance is fierce, but we are continually inching toward success. We have to have faith in that."

And as for Taina's contribution to this cause, she reasserted that she is "doing the best that I can during my time on this earth." For her, and for the rest of us, that is all any of us can ever offer, or hope for.

KIMBERLY SEALS ALLERS

"Whatever the question, the answer is in the community."
—KIMBERLY SEALS ALLERS, author and advocate
for maternal and infant health

I t's a Friday morning in October 2019 when I Skype with Kimberly Seals Allers in the midst of her busy travel schedule. She is flying to three different locations in the next four days. "I am catching a flight to Atlanta in two hours, then to DC tomorrow, and then to Australia on Monday," Kimberly tells me at the beginning of our interview. Nestled behind her beneath her kitchen's mahogany wood cabinetry is a sign that reads: RELAX. BELIEVE.

I usually find Kimberly professionally dressed in stylish and colorful capes and suits behind a pair of wide-rimmed, black-framed glasses, with her hair tied up in a bun, attending business meetings or events. But since she's at home, squeezing our interview in before she boards a plane, she looks relaxed in a dark blue sweatshirt. Her black hair hangs loose around her shoulders, and her white wire earphones dangle from behind her black hair. Still, her smile is bright, and her dark brown skin is glowing.

In Washington, DC, she'll serve as a judge for the National Academies of Medicine Public Health Care Challenge. After that she's flying to Australia, where she'll be speaking at a conference about healthy infant feeding. "Australia has a similar history of disparity to the US," she tells me. "Marginalized people have poor health outcomes due to that country's history of racism and bias in its healthcare system." Kimberly will be presenting two seminars there: "Speaking so you can be heard: Effective strategies for cross-cultural communication to dismantle breastfeeding barriers," and "Ethical community engagement in culturally and linguistically diverse communities." She will also be providing opportunities for one-on-one consulting on a topic she calls "Shifting strategies: Narrative change and strategic communications," where she challenges her clients to rethink the way they have been working to improve health outcomes and eliminate decades-long health disparities. "It is not a health problem," she says, "but a communications problem. Corporate culture can only be transformed by shifting how you talk about health and equity," she continues. "We need deep cultural engagement."

I first met Kimberly in February 2017, when we found ourselves standing side-by-side at a women's empowerment fundraiser in New York City. Kimberly formerly served as the editorial director of Women's eNews's Black Maternal Health Project under our organization's founder and previous executive director, Rita Henley Jensen.

When Kimberly introduced herself, I couldn't believe my good fortune. "I have been turning our office upside down looking for documentation to provide to the Kellogg Foundation that gave us the grant to support that project," I told her.

She responded with a huge smile, "I can provide you with all of the paperwork you need."

Later that year, Rita Henley Jensen passed away, and Women's eNews established an award in her name to pay tribute to her work and legacy. Kimberly was the most obvious choice to be the first recipient of this award, due to their joint effort to bring racial disparities in maternal healthcare to light. During her acceptance speech at our 2018 awards gala that May, Kimberly spoke about the pioneering work she and Rita had done together. They had published important pieces: "Black Women Are Dying! Enough Scaremongering, It's Time for Solutions," "The Problem With Alicia Keys, and Too Many Black Women Like Her," and "Memo to Michelle Obama: Big Food Makers Don't Give a Fructose About our Kids," focused on helping black women have healthy pregnancies and healthy babies by advocating for them to take more control over their own safety, nutrition, and medical treatment.

As an award-winning journalist, author of five books, and an international speaker on maternal and infant health, Kimberly's career has focused on birth, breastfeeding, and motherhood and its intersection with race, policy, and culture. Her fifth book, *The Big Letdown: How Medicine, Big Business, and Feminism Undermine Breastfeeding,* was published in January 2017. Taking us on a journey of the social, economic, and political influences of the breastfeeding culture in the US, the book's bright-yellow front cover features an image of a baby bottle filled with milk, with the nipple at the top tied into a knot.

"Why in the land where we boast about American exceptionalism do we suck at breastfeeding?" Kimberly asks in the book's introduction. She soon reveals the answer: "The messages we receive about breastfeeding are completely disconnected from the actual experience millions of women are having."

Kimberly then rolls her eyes. "Although hospitals tell new mothers that 'breast is best,' they are being sent home with formula 'just in case.' And while celebrities are being photographed nursing in public, other breastfeeding mothers are being asked to cover up in public."

She tells me that there is no one-size-fits-all answer: "Since breast-feeding provides the most benefits for mother and child, for those who are capable of doing so, it should be *the* feeding method of choice, regardless of the mother's race."

Kimberly is concerned about another crucial issue regarding childbirth, one that affects black mothers in particular. According to The Centers for Disease Control and Protection, the risk of pregnancy-related deaths for black women is three to four times higher than for their white counterparts.

"I had my first child days after completing my master's degree at Columbia University," she recalls. "At the hospital I was completely disrespected, my wishes were ignored, and I left feeling traumatized and violated." Researchers at Stanford University and others have documented treatment similar to what Kimberly experienced, citing implicit bias toward women of color, with 21 percent of black mothers and 19 percent of Hispanic mothers hospitalized for childbirth reporting perceptions of poor treatment due to race, ethnicity, cultural background, or language.

"I am on a mission to equalize the experience of giving birth in this country for every person," she says. She tells me about the new app she and her son recently created, called IRTH. "It's name comes from the word 'Birth,' but we dropped the b for bias," she says grinning. "I had this idea for an app that would collect and share hospital and physician reviews by patients, for the purpose of screening for racial bias." She enlisted her fifteen-year-old son, Michael, to take app development classes with her. He soon learned enough to create the original wireframes for the app. This mother–son project has since garnered a number of large grants in only a few months. "When we received our first grant, I had Michael come with me to the bank to deposit the check," she recalls. "It's important for a young black boy to see the results of his hard work. That's my favorite part, that my son can see he has an idea and then make it happen."

The app allows the user to enter a few personal details about herself and then look for a hospital or doctor review from someone like her. This empowers women to learn how someone with their racial identity, gender, religion, or income level has been treated by doctors or hospital staff.

"Reading a hospital review from a middle-class white woman does not necessarily help a low-income black woman," Kimberly says. While some people have expressed concern about what hospitals are going to say about it, Kimberly says that's not her concern. "Black women are dying," she says, "and if hospitals are serious about doing more than just providing anti-bias training, if they really want to have accountability and learn how this training is filtering down to patient experiences, this tool will be helpful to hospitals and doctors as well." She believes that hospitals and doctors may be well-intentioned, but that doesn't matter if women are dying. "If it's not working, we need to know," she says. "We need to harness our powers as consumers, and protect each other and our community."

Kimberly then talks proudly about how IRTH won a Media for Change Award at MIT's Media Lab "Make the Breast Pump Not Suck" hackathon on May 4, 2018, for addressing systemic gaps in postpartum support. Three foundation grants have since been awarded, totaling $300,000. The app will be released nationally in 2020, and Kimberly was excited to tell me that they'd just hired their first employee.

"Many industries need a disruption driven by consumer power, just like it worked for Uber and Airbnb." Kimberly turns off her stove and sits down to eat her breakfast. "We live in a consumer healthcare model, and it's time that we have it working for us, all of us."

She ends our interview with a quote from her book, which is printed on the tote bag she'd be carrying to the airport later that morning: "The revolution will not be individualized. It will be collective, connected, and rooted in community."

photo © Joan Lauren

LOREEN ARBUS

"Find your voice."

—Loreen Arbus, disability rights activist, philanthropist,
producer, writer, and author

"Find Your Voice." "Talk About Your Dreams." "Diversity."
"Justice" "Honesty" "Gratitude." "Kindness" "Inclusion."
These are just some of the many messages and words spray-
painted in bright multi-colors across the hallways, walls, and
windows in Loreen Arbus's New York City apartment. Why?
Because Loreen has a message to deliver—everywhere she goes
and in everything she does—and that's to inspire and raise
awareness for others, particularly for women and people with
disabilities. "Everywhere I go, it's never more than a second away
from me," she told me.

Her travels have taken her all over the world, mostly to
places where diversity and inclusion are already top priorities,
or where they should be. Gloria Steinem once said about Loreen,

"Wherever I am, if I see Loreen in the same room, I know I am in the right place."

Today I am sitting with Loreen in her New York City apartment on Central Park West. It's not the first time I've been to her home. I've visited dozens of times before, for any of the myriad of events she hosts and underwrites for organizations that are also committed to empowering women, girls, and the disabled. In fact, she has often said that she specifically chose this apartment and decorated it the way she has to provide a unique and memorable venue to support such organizations. And every time I enter her apartment, I see at least one thing I've never seen before.

Yes, there are the hand-painted crystal chandeliers, each a different color, hanging from the multicolored ceilings of each room. And, yes, there are the two tiny dogs who greet us, each dressed in a beautiful outfit selected from a wardrobe that would impress any fashionista. And, yes, the walls painted in pinks and yellows, blues and greens are a perfect backdrop to the many artists who visit, from the modern to the impressionist to the romantic. But Loreen will be the first to point out that she's not only interested in well-known artists, though she has acclaimed artists' work on her walls; indeed, she walks her talk—featuring artwork from people with disabilities, as well as street art.

"I love to buy art off the streets," she told me, "and I absolutely love showcasing artwork from artists who are disabled." She pointed to a rectangular painting of a linear black chair facing two square royal-blue windows placed on a bright pink wall above a sun-yellow floor. I hadn't seen this painting the last time I was at her apartment, though I did remember the painting of Judith Jameson, the renowned dancer and choreographer, painted by her father, that hangs just above it. I appreciate how both artists' works appear on the same wall, just inches from one another, commanding equal exposure.

To truly know the type of person Loreen is, you can take lessons from observing art because you also have to look closer at her as well. A lot closer. Don't be misled by her long sweeping black hair, often adorned with threads of jewels, or her long painted nails, which are flaming red the day of our interview, each fingernail embellished with a unique array of jewels, or her outfits, which are so brightly colored that she is often the most colorfully dressed person in a room—whether being photographed on the red carpet or speaking from a stage to a sold-out audience. Every detail is measured, and every word has meaning, since beneath the glamour and couture stands a woman who has devoted her work, and her life, to something very basic, heartfelt, and genuine: helping the marginalized.

I first met Loreen about eleven years earlier, when I wrote an article about her for *The Huffington Post*. The day before our scheduled interview, we coincidentally met at Gloria Steinem's seventy-fifth birthday party. I was wearing a bright-red jacket, and when I was introduced to her, she told me that I matched the color scheme of her apartment so well that I could "move right in." I showed up the next day with a suitcase as a joke.

Walking into Loreen's apartment for the first time is an experience. Colors of the rainbow stretch from floor to ceiling in every room, adorned by statues, paintings, and furniture that are as eclectic as they are unique. It was not a surprise to learn that she performed for years as a professional Argentine tango dancer all over the world, on Broadway and at the Hollywood Bowl, where dancers are commonly adorned in bright colors. The day of our interview she told me about her childhood, and how her father, Leonard H. Goldenson, was the founder and chair of what is today the world's largest media empire, Disney–ABC Television Group. Together with Loreen's mother, Isabelle, he also founded one of the largest health agencies in the US, United Cerebral Palsy. Her mother, specifically, created the concept of the telethon and originated the ideas enforcing federal mandates providing people with disabilities wheelchair-accessible sidewalks, public bathroom stalls, and public telephones, as well as handicapped parking spaces. These requirements were all created and developed because Loreen's older sister, Genise (nicknamed Cookie), was born with cerebral palsy. "I saw how she was marginalized, and it broke my heart," Loreen recalled, proud of the organization and the work her parents undertook to create a more supportive and loving environment for her sister, and all people with disabilities. "Most people would not talk to her, and the few who did spoke down to her," Loreen continued. "So much of what I've done in life has been prompted by watching how people behaved around her, and what my parents did to help her, and all people like her."

After we met, I went on to write two articles for *The Huffington Post* about Loreen, one in 2012 entitled "Turning Wheelchairs into Hot Rods," based upon Loreen's unrelenting support of children with cerebral palsy, which has enabled many to achieve beyond what was originally thought possible, and "Why Women Entrepreneurs Matter," which I wrote after attending Women's Entrepreneurship Day at the United Nations in November 2014, where Loreen was honored with its Philanthropy Pioneer Award.

"My father always said that I should never expect a handout," Loreen recalled in her acceptance speech. "He also said, 'The only thing that will truly matter one hundred years from now is how we touched the lives of others, and that is our immortality.'"

After becoming the executive director of Women's eNews in 2016, I also featured Loreen in our My Passion, My Philanthropy editorial series. In an article entitled, "Loreen Arbus: Work Defined by Marginalization," Loreen talked about her own personal challenges, marked by two opposing worlds: one of privilege and one of challenge. "I found myself marginalized at school because I was the only Jewish girl in an Episcopalian school. Despite being one of the best dancers in the school, I was placed in the back row for dance performances because of my religion." As she entered adulthood, she wanted a career in television.

"But," she said, "I didn't want to ride on my father's coattails, so I changed my last name to my maternal grandmother's name, Arbus." Loreen went on to become the first woman to head programming for a US network, a feat accomplished twice (both at Showtime and Cable Health Network/Lifetime).

I am a longtime admirer of Loreen's for all these reasons and more, which is why I contacted her to be interviewed for this book—prompting a third interview in September 2019. Once again, she made sure to devote the time to first talk about someone other than herself. As I sat down with her in her kitchen, her blue eyes fixed upon me. She was wearing red lipstick that matched her red painted nails; her long flowing black hair was gently tousled, reaching mid-waist. She was wearing a black blouse adorned by images of gray leaves, except at the bottom of her sleeves, where they appeared in bright red to match her lipstick and nails. She wore two silver rings, one on her left pointer finger in the form of a leaf to match her blouse, and another on the other pointer finger in the shape of a snail. Placed on the table in front of my chair was a printed tribute to Jessica Melore, a woman who had passed away just five days earlier at the age of thirty-seven. Jessica lived for twenty years with a heart transplant. She was a leg amputee and a three-time cancer survivor. Loreen showed me a photo of herself with Jessica taken less than one year earlier when Jessica was invited as Loreen's guest to a major women's empowerment celebration in New York City. "Can Women's eNews publish a tribute to Jessica," she asked me, her hand gently resting atop Jessica's printed obituary. "We can never be grateful enough for what we have. Every time I saw her, it drove that point home." We published Jessica's obituary in Women's eNews the next day.

Loreen then spoke about her sister, Cookie, who passed away in her twenties. "My sister inspired me," Loreen says. Her tone was soft and serious. "She had great depth but was very limited. She had very little dexterity, but everything she was able to do was so monumental; just to watch her wrap her fingers around a cup was an amazing moment." Loreen was pensive for a moment, seeming to be remembering her sister. "And she had a beautiful laugh," she says. Her caretaker, Miss Karen Hansen, was devoted to Cookie "twenty-five, eight," Loreen says. "She had pure love for my sister, unlike any I have ever experienced. I wish I had the capacity to love the way she did." Working tirelessly without complaint, Miss Hansen's one wish was that Cookie should not outlive her, to ensure that Cookie never experienced her passing. Miss Hansen passed away in her seventies, just six months after Cookie's death.

"Every philanthropic thing I do in my life is inspired by her memory," Loreen continues, referring to Miss Hansen. "She is always my guide." Loreen then lifts a piece of lemon from a Danish saucer, and places it in her tea. "I have a closet full of Danish china," she says, inviting me to follow her to a glass cabinet showcasing numerous pieces of blue-and-white dishes, cups, and saucers. "Miss Hansen was Danish, and every year for my birthday she gave me one piece of Danish china." She shows me the various pieces she has, smiling broadly as she recalls this family friend and caretaker to her sister.

Leading me back into her kitchen, she reminisces a bit more. "The first question I often ask people when I speak in public is, "Do you know who the largest minority in the world is?" Most don't know it's the disabled community. That's why Loreen has worked tirelessly over decades to raise awareness, from speaking about it at the United Nations; to serving as executive producer of *A Whole Lott More*, a 2014 documentary that focuses on the importance of hiring people with disabilities. She also awards disability awareness grants to seven organizations, including New York Women in Film and Television, to support female filmmakers with disabilities and female filmmakers who make films about disability issues. And there are countless other ways that Loreen has supported the visibility of people with disabilities. While serving as the founder and chair of the Women Who Care luncheon benefiting United Cerebral Palsy of New York City for fifteen years, for example, Loreen ensured that artwork created by children with cerebral palsy served as the centerpieces on every table. "Everything provides an opportunity to showcase their abilities," Loreen tells me. She was also the first person to introduce a woman in a wheelchair at Fashion Week in 2012.

Loreen then expresses one of her major current concerns, the intersection of women with disabilities and violence. "It is a huge phenomenon since these victims are defenseless and are often nonverbal," Loreen says. "It breaks my heart."

I then ask Loreen what her proudest achievement is thus far, and she tells me it's serving as cofounder of the Media Access Office, which increases employment, improves depiction, and raises consciousness regarding disability. "Employment of people with disabilities is so important," Loreen tells me. Her passion is clear as her voice gets a bit louder, her enthusiasm apparent. "The fascinating thing is that someone who hires a person with a disability is going to receive twice as much back, since that person is going to work much harder to prove that they can do the job, and do it well. Never underestimate the abilities of a person with a disability."

I then asked Loreen what her most poignant moment has been, and I am not surprised that she does not respond with an experience about herself, or anything she did. "It was at one of the Women Who Care luncheons when Dan Rather was presenting an award," she tells me. "I saw him talking with a young African American girl in a wheelchair offstage, and she told him her ambition was to open a beauty salon and only hire people with disabilities. He spent half an hour down on one knee talking with her. He was at her level."

As our interview comes to a close, Loreen escorts me to the front door, but not before I ask her about a new word I see spray-painted in green on a glass pane above the red kitchen door: MINIM, which refers to a musical term.

"I like this word because whether you read it forward or in reverse, it is exactly the same word," she tells me. "We need to look at people that way. No matter how they first appear to us, we are all equal."

photo © D. Finney Photography

DANIELLE BELTON

"I think the most meaningful thing I can do to normalize the conversation about mental illness is to just talk about it."

—DANIELLE BELTON, editor-in-chief, *The Root*

"One month I was in a mental hospital. The next month I moved to Washington, DC. And now here I am, working in the middle of Times Square," Danielle Belton said, almost disbelievingly. It was a hot summer day in July 2019 when I interviewed her at *The Root's* offices in the heart of New York City.

I first met Danielle at the annual Women's Media Center Awards Gala on November 1, 2018, a sold-out event at the lavish Capitale Ballroom in Manhattan's Little Italy, a historic building hailed for its colossal Corinthian columns, marble floors, and sixty-five-foot vaulted ceilings. A nonprofit organization created by Jane Fonda, Robin Morgan, and Gloria Steinem, the Women's Media Center's mission is to raise the visibility and viability of women and girls in the media, and that particular night leaders and champions for women in journalism were being honored. But there was one media powerhouse I was lucky enough to meet even before the celebratory dinner began, and she happened to be standing just to the right of me.

The room was already overflowing with hundreds of honorees, presenters, and attendees when I found myself standing next to Danielle Belton, the editor-in-chief of *The Root,* a celebrated digital news source providing black news, opinion, politics, and culture to millions of readers. Since assuming this position only two years earlier, Danielle had already helped increase *The Root's* monthly readership from 3.2 million to over 10 million by instilling, as she described it, "the journalistic merging of escapism with activism."

November also happened to be the month in which I was reviewing nominees for Women's eNews's annual 21 Leaders for the 21st Century Awards Gala, which takes place each May. I was on the lookout for someone to receive one very special award, The Rita Henley Jensen Award for Investigative Journalism, named in honor of our organization's founder. Rita was a journalist whose research and writing particularly focused on how our country's health services fail women of color. I thought of Danielle for the award that night, but it wasn't until I heard her acceptance speech at our gala six months later that I realized just how perfect a candidate she really was.

The Women's eNews Awards Gala took place on Monday, May 6, 2019, and Danielle took to the podium in a way that was overtly self-assured, almost shockingly so in light of what she was about to say. Instead of discussing journalistic accomplishments, she chose to share her most personal battles with mental health, and how she overcame numerous bouts of chronic sleeplessness and even suicidal ideation to stay alive. It was equally surprising that Danielle spoke in a voice that was decisive and direct, complemented by a stance that was commanding yet relaxed. One would normally not expect someone to address an audience of strangers in such a calm and composed manner, particularly when revealing her most personal battles with mental illness, which are still often considered taboo. Yet that is likely why the entire audience rose to its feet in applause at the end of her speech. *How many of these people have also experienced mental health hardships, or have had loved ones who have?* I wondered.

When I got together with Danielle a few weeks later, I asked about whether she considered the audience and how many other people were likely in the same boat, or knew someone who was.

"I want others who have similarly suffered to know that they can have lives as well," she told me.

She then spoke more specifically about her mental health history and how she got to this point of being in a position to help others. In December 2005, while working as an entertainment reporter in California, she was hospitalized at UCLA Medical Center, where she remained for two and a half weeks. Misdiagnosed with depression, she was placed on numerous medications, eventually prescribed a minimum of seven to ten pills per day. "I had tried every pill at that point," she said, until she was correctly diagnosed with bipolar disorder. "I was then put on one pill, lithium, the drug of choice for this condition," she told me.

"I then went back to my job, but I still wasn't feeling well," Danielle recalled. "Lithium made me feel super flat, so much so that I could no longer do my job." In 2007, she moved back to her parents' home in St. Louis, Missouri, which also meant returning to her bedroom in the basement. "In my mind, I didn't do anything for a year," Danielle said, shaking her head. "I felt completely dysfunctional and was preparing to give up on life." Ultimately, she was offered a job at a public relations firm. But after three months, she again felt depressed, and so she quit. "This was what continually happened to me," she said. "I would last all of three months at a job before I'd get super depressed, and then I'd leave."

This was when her love of writing saved her. "I missed writing so much that I started a blog called The Black Snob," Danielle recalled, shifting her eyes to look up at the ceiling. "It was supposed to serve as my alter ego, reflecting on race, mental health, politics, and culture." The timing couldn't have been more perfect. When Barack Obama won the Iowa Caucus in 2008, she had already been writing about race and politics, so she felt even more inspired to build an audience. "It was Christmas 2008, and I took a job at a local Macy's folding sweaters, cleaning dressing rooms, and tidying up racks, all the while writing about Michelle Obama and her fashion choices," she recalled. One of the first bloggers to write about Ms. Obama's style, Danielle was then invited to discuss the topic on major news outlets like Dateline, NPR, and The Associated Press. She was overcome shortly thereafter by bouts of depression and suicidality, as is typical of someone with bipolar disorder, even though she was taking her medication. That's when her older sister, Denise, took her to St. Mary's hospital to admit her for full time mental health care.

After spending about a week in the hospital, Danielle was invited to speak at a Black Policy Conference at Harvard University. Although yearning to go, she was terrified. "I had never been to the East Coast," she said. It was then that Danielle's mother spoke with the attending psychiatrist about it, and his response, Danielle said, was life-altering. "I think Danielle's problem is that she can't do nothing because that makes her sick, and doing too much also makes her sick," he said. This was the first time Danielle ever considered the possibility that she could work, but also rest in between. "It never occurred to me that I could do both," she reflected amusedly.

She did go to Harvard to speak at the conference, and received what she described as overwhelmingly positive feedback. "I was the rock star on my panel," she recalled. From then on, she became fully energized and obsessed with moving to the East Coast—first to Washington, DC, then to New York City.

Yet Danielle's mental health would soon be challenged again, not once, but twice. Her close friend, Toya Watts, whom she met while working in DC, died from colon cancer at age forty-eight in 2014. Then Danielle's mother, diagnosed with dementia in 2013, passed in 2018. "But when she passed," Danielle told me, "it helped me realize that I needed to live my life because nothing is guaranteed."

It was in 2015, while still reeling from her mother's memory loss and her friend's death, that she contacted *The Root* and asked for a full-time job, even though she was still feeling depressed. She was offered a position as associate editor, and within a year was promoted to managing editor. "When I was offered the managing editor position, I almost didn't take it," Danielle recalled. "My friends had to remind me of who I was and what I could do." Looking back, she believes this job saved her life, she told me, "because I realized I had to be responsible for more than myself, for other people who reported to me."

Now leading *The Root's* editorial team as its editor-in-chief, she ensures that coverage of mental health issues is front and center. Whether it be by publishing articles about the struggles of the famous, as was the case in the August 2018 article entitled "Serena Williams Just Got Real—and Relatable—About Postpartum Emotional Fallout," or about the struggles of Black people in general, as in the May 2018 piece, "It's OK Not to Be OK: 2 Black Teens Use Tech to Prevent Suicide," or when Danielle posted a piece about her own battles in May 2019 in an article called "Being Bipolar Means Always Having to Say, 'Um . . . What's Your Name Again?'" Danielle is using her experiences to impart knowledge, courage, and persistence, hoping this will help others as much as it has helped her.

"I used to think about death every day, but now I can't remember the last time I thought about dying," Danielle told me. "Instead, I now focus on living."

And she is now writing a book, a humorous book entitled *Bipolar Logic,* to help remove some of the stigma surrounding this disorder. "Bipolar is scary, but those who have it need to learn that it's a condition you live with." Her major concern is that too many people who are diagnosed with it are "in the closet," so Danielle wants them to see that she has an important job, a family, and many friends, even though, as she says, "I just happen to have this." As our interview comes to a close, she sits forward in her chair, her eyes beaming with hope and positivity. "Life is good now, because I found compassion, love, and patience for myself." She also said she learned how to make peace with herself and live with this disease viewing both as "a mystery and a mixed blessing, sometimes fueling my creativity, but always making me more in tune with the world around me."

photo © David Handschuh

KRISTEN PRATA BROWDE

"White male privilege is real."

—KRISTEN PRATA BROWDE, attorney and the first transgender
candidate to be endorsed by a major political party in New York State

It is rare for a person, any person, to experience what it is like
to be treated both as a male and a female in society. Kristen
Prata Browde is one of those people.

I first learned about Kristen in the spring of 2017. I had
invited a friend of hers, Carol Evans, the former CEO/founder of
Working Mother Media and cofounder of Executive Women for
HER, to be interviewed on *Women's eNews Live*, a radio show I
launched to further introduce women's progressive voices to the
public. She was familiar with my show, especially as a resident
of Chappaqua, a small hamlet in the town of New Castle, New
York, where it was broadcast. Immediately following the interview, she sent me an email: "You must also interview Kristen
Browde," she wrote. "She's running for town supervisor of New

Castle, and is the first transgender candidate to be endorsed by a major political party in New York State."

I contacted Kristen, and she agreed to call in as a guest a few weeks later. We first talked about Chappaqua itself, and how it's known as the home base for such national political power-houses as Secretary of State Hillary Clinton and President Bill Clinton, as well as Congressman Horace Greeley. Referring to the importance of local elections like town supervisor, however, Kristen said, "We need to take back this country starting at the town level, and working one town at a time."

Although Kristen didn't win that 2017 election, it did not put an end to her political pursuits. In fact, she was now running for the New York State Assembly. I asked her if she could take some time out of her busy election campaign to be interviewed again, this time in person as a change-maker for this book.

I drove to her house in Chappaqua on January 15, 2020, where her cleaning woman answered the door and escorted me to the living room. As I waited for Kristen, I noticed a framed certificate naming one of her two sons, Theo, as a champion in the 2017 Macbook Music Madness Mixmaster, alongside a framed headshot of him. Standing to the left were two Emmy awards Kristen had won in her previous career as a news correspondent, which she wrapped up in 2013 after a sixteen-year stint with CBS News. Kristen is now the principal of Browde Law, PC, a law practice that focuses on divorce and family law. She is also the president of the LGBT Bar Association of Greater New York and cochair of the National Trans Bar Association.

Kristen walked in wearing a simple gray top and black pants. Her hair and makeup looked freshly done, and she explained that her photographer was arriving after our interview to shoot her new campaign photos. I asked her why she decided to run for the New York State Assembly. "After my younger son came home one day from his second mandatory lockdown drill at his high school, I had a conversation with him. I realized that his generation is growing up with the belief and fear that their school is going to be next. This is the sad and unacceptable reality our kids live in," she said. "It was quickly apparent that the best way to cut into that fear was that instead of cajoling our legislators to do what we want, we have to become the legislators to do what we want."

Kristen has experienced gun violence firsthand. She was working as a correspondent in the CNN Washington, DC, bureau office the day President Ronald Reagan was shot in 1981, and was one of the first reporters on the scene. "Gun owners have to understand that we don't want to take their guns away, that we don't want to interfere with people who use guns for hunting, or even for self-protection. But since the men in Washington have made it plain that they are not going to protect New Yorkers, we need to protect ourselves, and the place I can do the most good is in the state legislature." She then pointed out that "the men in politics are not all bad guys, but they don't have the passion or the correct perspective to do what's right." I asked her to lay out for me her campaign vision, which is based on a platform for legislative action in Albany, New York, on issues starting with common-sense gun and ammunition legislation, dealing with the Trump-enabled rise in hate crimes, and ending discrimination against women, starting with the pink tax, where products with the same ingredients and materials are sold at higher prices to women than to men. "Could you imagine," Kristin said, "that one week I am paying four dollars for my shirt to be washed and pressed and the next week, as a woman, I have to pay twice that much?"

Kristen spoke passionately about how gender stereotypes tend to steer people away from displaying qualities that would enable men to be more sensitive about issues like gun violence. "Men are not supposed to, and often don't, display empathy, compassion, or tenderness," she argued. "They also need to learn to listen as opposed to talking most of the time. In the past, women have allowed men to talk over us, but that's not happening anymore. We need to push back against that stereotype and allow people, no matter their assigned sex at birth, to be more empathetic and take feelings into consideration."

She referred to universal healthcare as an example. "The traditional male believes that if you can't afford it, you can't have it. In contrast, when Hillary Clinton first ran for Senator of New York, she talked about healthcare as a fundamental right for families. We've had men running things in this country for more than two hundred years," she said, now moving forward in her chair, "but viewing healthcare as a fundamental right has either never occurred to them, or they just don't care."

Having been a male in this society, and now a female since 2016, Kristen knows what she speaks of when she reflects on the incredible privilege she had growing up. "I was seen as a white man who was Ivy-League educated. I was handed privilege by luck of heritage, which had nothing to do with me. And I can tell you, white privilege is real, particularly male white privilege."

She then told me how different it was to be treated first as a man in the business world, and then as a woman. "Before I came out, I would walk into a politician's office, or be in a news conference, and when I asked a question, there was no doubt that the male politician, seeing me as a male reporter, was going to deal with me and my question respectfully. Since I came out as a woman, the responses are different. When I am in court, most male attorneys, seeing a female attorney on the other side, try to talk over me, without the slightest hesitation or fear." Recalling the first time this happened to her, she said it was "super jarring." She recalled, "I never experienced that before. Fortunately, having previously experienced male privilege I wasn't putting up with it. I responded very abruptly in a way I wish more women would do, because the man who tried to talk over me for the better part of the morning eventually backed off. But for men, that instinct is there," she continued. "Men will try to steamroll women in business, law, and politics."

I asked her about how it felt to very publicly transition from male to female. "Coming out as transgender is much like jumping out of an airplane with no parachute, only to discover you have wings," she responded, sporting a wide grin. "All you have to do is reduce the fear, and jump!"

She then turned on her phone and showed me a photo of her wearing a form-fitting, silver mid-length dress with black pumps, standing front and center with twenty-five white men standing all around her. "In 2018, I went to my fiftieth high school reunion in St. Louis. They were quite certain that it was an all-boys school half a century ago," she told me, letting out a loud laugh. "I was planning to attend, but debated if I should let everyone know of my transition in advance, or just spring it on them. I decided to alert the class secretary. The email I wrote to him was included in the Alumni Newsletter, so everyone knew before I arrived. Still, I kept being steered to the girls' school anniversary party, which was the same night. In the end, everyone was terrific, even though one or two of my fellow graduates gave me dirty looks. But their wives were great," she added.

I asked Kristen why she decided to practice family law instead of remaining a news correspondent. "First," she said, "it allowed me to have a more reliable schedule to be there for my sons, whom I needed to prepare for school and take care of after. Secondly, I'm pretty good at getting people to consensus. Imagine taking two people who once loved each other but who now can't agree on anything, and getting them to a place where they agree again. And this is not so different from the way to gain consensus politically. We have Democrats who support an overall platform but can't agree on what the agenda should be. It takes coalitions, and I am pretty good at creating them."

Kristen shared her thoughts about how the Democratic party has been changing dramatically, with more progressives being elected to office, particularly women. "We are now seeing the last vestiges of the traditional male-dominated party, which is being swept away, not in a negative way, but by the force of women who are doing things like organizing and getting the voters out to the polls. This is the political power that can really change the world!"

She then reverted to use her suburban New York district as an example. "In this little assembly district, 61 percent of the voters in the most recent primaries were women. These women are awake. It matters to us, and it matters to our families. Women are a political force," she said, "and if male politicians don't figure that out, they will be unemployed, or they ought to be."

Kristen's photographer arrived after a while and began setting up for her photo shoot. "You know, if I win this election I will be just one of a total of one-hundred-fifty assembly members. But the other one-hundred-forty-nine will definitely know I'm there. After all, when it comes to making change, it's pretty obvious that's something I know about."

photo © Margaret Randall

BLANCHE WIESEN COOK AND CLARE COSS

"Never go anywhere without your gang!"

—Blanche Wiesen Cook, historian, author,
and professor of history

It was a clear, starlit evening in July 2019 when I walked to the New York Historical Society on Manhattan's Upper West Side, located directly across from Central Park. I was looking forward to attending the sold-out event, "Coconspirators: An Evening with Blanche Wiesen Cook and Clare Coss." Blanche is a historian, professor, and author of numerous books, including a three-volume biography of Eleanor Roosevelt. Clare, psychotherapist emeritus, is a librettist and award-winning playwright. They first met in 1966 at a meeting of the Women's International League for Peace and Freedom called to organize an action against the war in Vietnam.

As I entered the museum and found my way to the room where the discussion was being held, I noticed a large rectangular cake sitting on a table just outside the entrance door. In colorful lettering on white frosting, it read: *Happy 50th Anniversary.* Blanche and Clare had been partners in life for fifty years.

For the next ninety minutes, the audience listened intently. Blanche first spoke about the women who inspired her. "Our gang in the seventies was amazing," she said. That gang included renowned poet, essayist, and feminist Adrienne Rich and civil rights activist and poet Audre Lorde, whose awe-inspiring quotes include, "Your silence will not protect you." Blanche recalled, "They were both my guides at the time. We were all in it together, protesting to end the Vietnam War. It was an electrifying time."

Clare talked about two women who inspired her commitment to activism and equal justice. First was Lillian Wald, founder of the Henry Street Settlement and the Visiting Nurse Service in 1893, and the Neighborhood Playhouse in 1916—all three vibrant New York institutions to this day. "Wald's vision and activism to work for international peace and to bring education, sanitation, playgrounds, health care, school lunches, and the arts to the Lower East Side served as a model for the country," she said. In her research on Wald, she discovered another inspiration, Mary White Ovington, cofounder of the National Association for the Advancement of Colored People (NAACP) in 1909. "She was the first white woman in the early 1900s to dedicate her life to racial justice."

They also recognize and appreciate how they have inspired each other over the decades. "Clare is the leader of my personal gang," Blanche said. "Her brilliance inspires and informs all my work."

"Blanche is bold and unafraid of confrontation or disagreement and always speaks truth to power. She taught me a lot on that score," Clare responded.

I was touched by this conversation, seeing their dedication to their causes as well as to each other. And interviewing them in their home two months later only reinforced their authentic commitment to their work and to one another.

Clare greeted me at the door as soon as I arrived. It was October, and she was dressed for fall in black and gray. Her white hair hung softly just above her shoulders, framing her bangs which stop just above her small, round, unframed eyeglasses. Their home is filled with books and memorabilia, particularly photos of Eleanor Roosevelt. "I call her 'the other woman,'" Clare said with a wide grin. After I followed Clare into the living room, Blanche entered, and we sat to talk. Blanche has salt-and-pepper, short curly hair, and she was clothed in western wear: blue jeans and red cowgirl boots. Blanche and Clare immediately held hands. Blanche is seventy-eight years old, and Clare recently turned eighty-four.

On a full moon in June 2019, their chosen anniversary month, they celebrated their fiftieth year together. On their fortieth anniversary, they "eloped" to Martha's Vineyard for a small private wedding on a friend's deck overlooking the bay. Gay marriage had just become legal in Massachusetts. "July 11 is the tenth anniversary of our marriage," Clare said.

"We were each married to men when we met. After three years of courtship, shared activism, and intense passion, we left our husbands to live together," Blanche shared.

As an activist and playwright, Clare believes we all "have the power to create a just world," and has written one-woman plays about her mentors: Lillian Wald and Mary White Ovington. "Their steady, embracing, and fierce commitment to justice deepened and informed my own activism," Clare said. In October 2020, the new opera, *Emmett Till*, which composer Mary Watkins set to Clare's libretto, will premiere at John Jay College's Gerald W Lynch Theater. Presented in association with John Jay, Opera Noire of NY, and The Harlem Chamber Players, the libretto narrates the horrific murder of a fourteen-year-old African American Chicago boy, Emmett Till, who was kidnapped, tortured, and murdered in the Mississippi Delta in 1955 for allegedly wolf-whistling at a white woman. Mamie Till-Mobley insisted on an open casket so the world could see what happened to her son, and courageously testified at the trial under death threats. Photos of this image appeared in hundreds of magazines and newspapers around the country and the world, placing a spotlight on his tragic death and the racism that caused it. Roanne Taylor, the teacher (a character Clare introduces), represents white folks who care but remain silent. Her dramatic arc travels from denial to the recognition of responsibility. "Mary Watkins and I have collaborated through five years of development workshops and sing-throughs," Clare said. "My play, *Emmett Down in My Heart*, which inspired the opera, will have a production in German by an Afro-German theater troupe, Label Noir, in December 2020 in Berlin."

At that point Clare graciously turned toward her partner, and Blanche talked about her work. Blanche has fought for women's rights, sexual freedom, and peace. As cofounder of the Freedom of Information and Accountability Committee (FOIA), she kept the Freedom of Information Act alive and fought to keep government records publicly accessible. "When I was working on my book, *The Declassified Eisenhower,* everything I wanted was classified," she said. "I asked for papers about Iran and Guatemala, and everything was secret. When the library trays were wheeled to me, they were all empty." That's what led to her founding FOIA, which provides the public with the right to receive any records requested from federal agencies. "I flew out of Abilene to New York to call a meeting of historians, journalists, attorneys—members of the Center for Constitutional Rights and American Civil Liberties Union. We founded FOIA, Inc. Bella Abzug was in Congress, and she worked to get a Freedom of Information Act passed which guaranteed the public's right to know—which remains embattled to this day." Blanche's book *The Declassified Eisenhower* was published in 1981. Ronald

Reagan sought to reclassify many of the documents that we got declassified, and the battle against secrecy has intensified."

While conducting research for her biographies of Eleanor Roosevelt, she was shocked to find that Eleanor's FBI file was so large. "Over five thousand pages," Blanche said, seemingly still in disbelief over this fact. "Eighty percent of her file is about her battles against lynching and racist terror. And J. Edgar Hoover hated her. He called her a 'fat cow.'" She continued though she seemed ruffled now, as Eleanor Roosevelt is clearly her biggest hero and inspiration. "Hoover was a monster. He considered anyone who fought for peace and wanted to end poverty communists. He even called Jane Addams, who fought for women's suffrage and advocated for world peace, the most dangerous woman in America in the year of her death, 1935."

The more Blanche researched Eleanor Roosevelt, the more she discovered what a visionary she was, a woman who led with her heart. "Her great vision was her love for all people and her ability to empathize and communicate with everyone," Blanche told me.

"We need more of that today," Clare concurred. I noticed that the two of them were still holding hands, and was touched by their clear affection. "We both are dedicated to help make the world a better place." She then referred to a quote by Annette T. Rubinstein, the renowned educator, author, and activist who passed at the age of ninety-seven in 2007. "Life is about the struggle." Blanche nodded in agreement. "We feel a mandate to try to work for justice, gender equality, dignity, and respect for everyone," Blanche added. "Our relationship keeps refueling us."

Blanche turned the conversation to the present challenges we face. "It is so terrible all over the world. During the 1960s we hoped money would be transferred from military spending to addressing people's needs. The SALT agreements, developed to restrain the arms race and limit nuclear weapons, were even signed by the USA and the USSR in the early 1970s. But now these agreements have been abandoned."

Clare added, "The only way to keep from getting depressed is to keep active. Write a letter. Make a phone call. Sign a petition. Call a meeting. Organize. Demonstrate out on the streets. Do whatever you're capable of doing. That's why we write. I am drawn to characters in my writing who break the silence and act.

Clare asks herself, "What would Lillian Wald do? What would Mary White Ovington do? What would Eleanor do? Hey—what would Blanche do?" Blanche added, "What would Clare do?"

photo © Gerald Peart

ALICE DEAR

"You need someone to have your back, and
you need to guard the back of others."

—ALICE DEAR, former ambassador to
the African Development Bank

I met Alice Dear in the summer of 2013 when I was serving as the board chair at Women's eNews. Its founder and executive director, Rita Henley Jensen, was hoping to add a board member with experience in the international business world. Due to Alice's success as an international business consultant, we felt she would be an ideal addition. The three of us met for lunch in the Woolworth Building, directly across from Women's eNews headquarters in downtown Manhattan.

Rita and I were already seated at a table in the back corner of the restaurant when Alice walked in dressed in bold African prints, reflecting years spent as a businesswoman in Africa. When we first tried to recruit her, she'd seemed somewhat taken aback, responding that she already had a full plate, particularly since she was in the midst of writing her memoir. We asked her again, toward the end of our lunch. "Your expertise in the global community is crucial to the expansion of our content abroad," I added. She then agreed to join us, since her international work was so close to her heart.

As I came to know Alice over the next few months, I better understood that joining the board had to do with living her values. "You need someone to have your back, and you need to guard the back of others. That's what women do," she once told me.

Alice's expertise in the international business world spanned more than thirty years, including eleven years on Wall Street as an international lending officer, and as an appointee by President Bill Clinton in 1994 serving as the US executive director of the African Development Bank. For the six years she held this position (1994–2000), she represented the US Government on the Board of Directors of the African Development Bank, headquartered in Abidjan, Cote d'Ivoire. She later served as vice president of the African Millennium Fund LLC, an overseas private investment corporation-sponsored private equity fund where she designed the Women and Small Business Initiative.

When I resigned as Women's eNews board chair at the end of 2013, the organization was preparing for a transition in leadership in anticipation of the founder's retirement. Alice was the only board member willing to take over as chair. It was not the case that more time had opened up in her schedule. Once again, she "had our back," making the needs of the organization a priority, even above her own.

It wasn't until three years later, in February 2016, that I ran into Alice again, at the Global Summit of Women Gala in Washington, DC, where she was serving on its Advisory Council. And then three months later at the Women's eNews annual gala honoring 21 Leaders for the 21st Century, where Rita Henley

Jensen announced her resignation as its executive director to pursue other endeavors. Alice was there again, and this time I invited her to meet over lunch the following week.

During lunch I told her that I was interested in rejoining Women's eNews as a board member. Alice confided how difficult the leadership transition had become with Rita's departure and the interim executive director's contract about to expire. I now offered to step in and help.

"I can do all of this for you," I told Alice. She looked up from her plate, dropped her fork, and breathed a huge sigh of relief, while again displaying a wide grin. Immediately following our lunch, we put the plan in motion.

I was installed as executive director fewer than two months later in July. It wasn't an easy time. Alice had already told me that the organization was in debt, and she was giving me six months to make it profitable, or it would be shut down. As someone who welcomes challenges, I was undeterred, and I put my creativity into motion. A critical decision to close our head-quarters helped to strengthen our future, and I soon paid off all debt and made the organization profitable by launching a radio show, *Women's eNews Live*, which provided us with a new and successful revenue stream. We have remained profitable ever since and Alice has remained board chair.

Four years later I called Alice and asked if I could interview her for this book. We spoke in January 2020.

Every time I see Alice, she is wearing something reminiscent of her fifty years of travel experiences in Africa. On the day of our interview, she showed me five thin bracelets circling her wrist. "These are made from elephant hair," she said, as she rotates the bracelets with her left hand. "It's supposed to bring good luck, and bless the wearer with health, love, and prosperity."

I wonder whether Alice needs any luck. She's the kind of woman who makes her own by giving to others and receiving support in return. When I asked her to share some of her backstory, she told me, "I left banking to start an international consulting business focused on Africa with my first client, a broker–dealer firm started by two friends I knew from our days as college students at Howard University. I positioned them to be chief underwriters for a large African Development Bank bond issue. Over the next several years, I sought opportunities to grow my consulting business with international institutions, such as UN agencies, the World Bank, and the African Development Bank. Fast forward four years to May 1992. I was in Senegal attending the African Development Bank's annual meeting. I had dinner with a small group that included David Bloomgarden, the advisor to the US executive director. As the topic turned political, and to that year's upcoming US presidential campaign, he lamented that if the Republicans were to lose, his boss would have to start searching for another job. With no forethought, my natural response was, 'Tell your boss to find another job!'" Alice now breaks out into a loud laugh, still delighted by her spontaneous response.

Soon after Bill Clinton was elected president, Alice received a call from a former international banker friend in New York who was then Washington-based and active in the private sector. "To my surprise, he asked for permission to recommend me to President-elect Clinton's transition team for a position in the administration," she recalled. Although her experience was ideal, there was someone who was intent on standing in her way: Larry Summers, then deputy secretary of the treasury. He was adamant that his candidate would be the next US director and sought to undermine Alice during the vetting process. Summers was also the former president of Harvard University who received a lot of backlash in 2005 after saying that there may be innate, biological differences between men and women that explained why fewer women succeed in science and math careers.

"Larry attempted to sabotage me with his claim that the treasury did not have a good relationship with the AfDB president, and because I was a close friend to the president, I was a problem," Alice told me. "But I told him that he was looking at the situation in the wrong way: What Larry was characterizing as my weakness was actually my strength—as a close friend to the president, I would have his ear."

Alice then called on her international network of sisters from Alpha Kappa Alpha sorority to reach out to the White House on her behalf. They lit up the switchboard. "This is yet one more example of the critical importance of other women having your back, but it also must be built before the need is there," Alice said. "I have been a member of AKA since my sophomore year at Howard University, where the sorority was founded in 1908. These are the ladies I sat on the floor with when Howard students took over the administration building in 1968, initiating student protests that quickly followed at Columbia University and several others. These are the ladies I have bonded with, and continue to bond with, for over fifty years." In fact, when Alice's graduating class celebrated its fiftieth class reunion in May 2019, she helped them raise over one million dollars in merit-based scholarship funds for the Howard University Class of 1969's reunion gift. This gift is helping Howard's students who are in need of financial support.

Further, as a banker, Alice was an active member of the Urban Bankers' Coalition, and witnessed the benefits of this network as well. "Over the years I have been associated with several women's organizations and allied with community-based organizations, and the give and take, the learning and sharing of knowledge and experiences has helped all of us grow and blossom into our best selves," she continued. "None of us can make it alone."

LAUREN EMBREY

*"I don't understand why people
feel they need a billion dollars."*

—LAUREN EMBREY, philanthropist

"I don't understand why people feel they need a billion dollars," Lauren Embrey tells me as we sit down for her interview at a trendy boutique hotel in New York City's West Village neighborhood. Lauren had flown in from her hometown of Dallas, Texas, for a number of meetings with nonprofit boards on which she serves. The hotel's lobby is as iconic as it is eclectic. A 1950s L.C. Smith & Bros. manual typewriter sits on one long vertical table alongside a round table where *Time Out New York*, *IN New York*, and *Where New York Traveler* magazines showcase the nightlife, culture, and entertainment in this bustling neighborhood. Three rows of Andy Warhol photos, identical but in different colors, grace the mahogany wall behind the registration desk.

Lauren arrives wearing all black, sporting a chic short hair-cut, her chestnut-brown round-rimmed eyeglasses matching her hair color. She appears trim, poised, and proper. The two ear-rings she's wearing do not match. "I like surprising people," she says. "It opens them up to thinking in a different way."

Lauren was born into a "wealthy southern upbringing," as she describes it, the youngest of two daughters. Her father was a successful real estate developer. After speaking for a while about her background, she tells me that her partner is an artist from El Paso, TX. "It has been challenging bridging our cultures and upbringings, mine wealthy southern in the 1960s, his Chicano in the 1970s, but we have learned a lot from one another. It has deep-ened our character and understanding of others," Lauren said.

In 2004, Lauren's father established a family foundation. Although he was already giving personally, the foundation was a way to not only formalize his giving but also to determine how much of his estate he wanted to dedicate to philanthropy and how much he wanted to pass on to future generations. "From inception, we worked together as a family, and very little was in the corpus until after his death one year later, in 2005. That is when the money started coming in . . . his formal documents had no restrictions on what to give to or where . . . so it was open for my sister and me to decide," Lauren said. One of the first decisions the foundation made was to fund and help build the Embrey Human Rights Program at Southern Methodist University. "I will never forget the first human rights course I took during my graduate studies," Lauren recalls. "I was stunned to learn about the litany of atrocities that have occurred around the world, most of which I was not aware of, but most stunning to me was learning about America's involvement in many of these atrocities," she continued. "I feel learning about human rights earlier would have planted a seed for my passion and my career path had this been a part of my undergraduate education." Today, the program at SMU is one of only a handful to grant a bachelor's degree in human rights education, and the only one in the South.

To hear Lauren tell her story is to learn that her penchant for breaking barriers started when she was very young. In an article that appeared in Women's eNews on August 9, 2016, where Lauren was a subject in our My Passion, My Philanthropy series profiling outstanding female philanthropists, Lauren talked about her childhood: "When I was young, I wanted to drive a moped, but was told I couldn't because I was a girl. I did not understand this. When I got older, I was invited to train for the Olympics in swimming, but my mother's response was, 'Why would you want green hair and big shoulders?' I didn't understand that either. Then at the elite girls' school I attended in Dallas, my hometown, the message changed. I was taught that I could accomplish anything any man could. I was not to consider myself 'lesser' in any regard, and definitely not because of my gender."

This was only the beginning of what would result in her life-altering change. "My parents divorced after my sophomore year in high school," she tells me now. Although she was still attending the private school, Lauren decided to change to the public school in her area in order to, as she put it, "See the real world." Her mother moved to San Francisco, and although Lauren continued to live primarily with her father in Dallas, she visited her mother often. This enabled Lauren to experience the culture there from the early seventies to mid-eighties. "My mom took me to drag shows, and I was immersed in the hip cross-cultural community of that time," she continued.

Stepping out into "the real world" was what reinforced her determination to support the rights of others. The official motto of the Embrey Human Rights Program at Southern Methodist University is "There is no such thing as a lesser person," and Lauren lives these words through her support of human rights.

In 2008, when the Dallas Women's Foundation was running a multimillion-dollar capital campaign, they asked Lauren to support their work with a grant of $250,000. Lauren knew that Women Moving Millions, a nonprofit organization that supports gender equality as a human right, was growing due to the involvement and leadership of the Women's Funding Network, of which the Dallas Women's Foundation was a part. Lauren proposed a much larger amount, one million dollars, to her board, which the board approved. Lauren then notified the Dallas Women's Foundation that they would not be making a gift of $250,000. "Instead, I was able to tell them we would be contributing one million," Lauren says with a huge smile. "I wanted to be a part of this incredible group of women that were making bold statements with their money. I wanted to do the same."

This initial gift connected Lauren to a broader community of individuals investing in women and girls, and, she says, "helped me realize how badly they need money." Her million-dollar investment in this sector has since grown to donating over $12 million in aid of projects that support women and girls.

Lauren recalls that in 2010, due to the continuing recession, she learned that a lot of philanthropic giving was moving backward at a time when suffering was increasing. "I proposed to our foundation's board that we embrace a new mantra: 'Give Big and Bold . . . Now.' We got the board to approve an initiative named Mission Without Borders that would support initiatives that drive systemic change in five areas: human rights education and awareness, women and girls' leadership, racial and gender equity, art for social change, and domestic human trafficking." This initiative would last from 2010 to 2014 and put over $15 million dollars out into the world.

Just one week before our interview, Lauren spoke about the importance of giving to a room filled with over three hundred women and men upon receiving an award from the Women's Media Center. Yet she also announced that her foundation was sunsetting and will therefore be putting all of its money out into the world over the next few years. She spoke about what was next for her, telling the room, "I am enshrined in a wonderful feeling of connectedness, but at the same time disturbed by the systems of separateness that surround us. I want a way out!" she said. Embracing what may lie ahead, she quoted Rabbi Abraham Heschel, who said, "It can be an ecstasy of deeds, luminous moments in which we are raised above our will, moments filled with outgoing joy, with intense delight."

For Lauren this is a season of not knowing, and she's okay with that. She tells me that she "must live into this unknowing." She recalls what Maya Angelou said at the inauguration of President Bill Clinton in 1993:

> "Here, on the pulse of this new day, you may have the grace to look up and out
> And into your sisters' eyes, and into your brothers' face,
> Your country, and simply say, very simply, with hope:
> Good Morning."

Lauren acknowledges that, while the specifics of her next stage of life are still unclear, she knows it will continue to involve providing resources for change. "But not just capital resources," she says. "It will provide human and knowledge resources as well. Resources grounded in heart and compassion. To come to any challenge as a partner with deep involvement, true listening, and total commitment. That will always be my conviction."

KAREN HAYCOX

"We build walls that matter!"

—KAREN HAYCOX, CEO of Habitat for
Humanity New York City

"You have to follow the pebbles of opportunity," Karen Haycox says. "You never know where they will lead you." Growing up in Canada, "just an inch north" of Detroit on the Canadian side of the Ontario–Michigan border, she always wanted to be Mary Tyler Moore, the iconic actress who played a television news producer on an Emmy-award winning sitcom of the 1970s. This led to an early career as a producer, but instead of working in the newsroom, she produced commercials for General Motors and Coca-Cola. "I was keeping the world a safe place for bright shiny metals and brown fizzy drinks," she says with a laugh. Following another pebble of opportunity, she had a short stint as a recruiter, where she placed a candidate for a senior position with Habitat for Humanity, which also landed Karen on its board of directors. This opened the door for her to later be hired as executive director of a local affiliate.

Fast forward fifteen years, and Karen is now the CEO of Habitat for Humanity, New York City, a nonprofit housing developer that builds and preserves affordable homes alongside families in need. Today, we are sitting in her downtown Manhattan office surrounded by memorabilia from a career that includes a variety of senior leadership roles across the organization. "Before I joined Habitat, the only things I knew about it, like most people, were that it was started by President Jimmy Carter, and that they give away homes," she says with a chuckle. "Neither of which is true."

It's November 2019 when I sit in Karen's office for this interview. She appears relaxed in a loose-fitting, long-sleeved black shirt and black pants, and her fashionably cut, short silver-gray hair paints a striking picture. She is seated behind her desk, surrounded by photos of people who have been helped through the work of her organization.

It wasn't until she began working with Habitat for Humanity that she found a deeper fulfillment in her work, when, as she describes it, a hole she didn't know was there was finally filled. "The homes we provide are like springboards, and the impact is like ripples in ponds," she says. "It's about so much more than just structures." All of the photos sitting in frames on her desk, office cabinet, and window ledges feature trips Karen has taken, where she's built onsite, alongside families in need. There is a photo of two little boys playing in the street of southern India just after the Tsunami hit there in 2004.

"Here's one of a little girl in Romania," she says, pointing to a photo of a five-year-old. "We were building a home there for her family at the time," she says. Karen then lifts a photo of a woman she met in Lonavala, India. "She didn't speak a word of English," she recalls. "When the building was completed, this woman, who wasn't even five feet tall, parted the crowd and walked right up to me. She reached up and held my face in her hands and then touched her heart. Then she did it again, holding my face and then touching her heart," Karen recalls, her eyes welling up at the memory. "It was a profound moment," she continues. "She was thanking me through the language of her heart, and that sustains me to this day."

What's meaningful about Habitat for Humanity is that "we provide a hand up, not a handout, to the families we work with." Working with the organization for over twenty years, Karen has a rolodex of images in her mind of all the families she's worked with, and, in particular, the faces of the children when they see their homes completed.

In Haiti, Karen witnessed women picking up plastic bottles from the garbage in an effort to bring money in for the family. She watched a mother in India who brushed her daughter's hair every morning while they were living on the street and sleeping in front of a hotel. "Each morning they would fold everything up and leave before they were kicked out," she recalls. "Those mothers have the same hopes and dreams that anyone has for their children."

Similar stories exist more locally in the streets of New York City. "The families we serve are doing everything right, like working full-time jobs to open the city in the morning and close it at night, yet they still struggle to afford even basic housing and wouldn't even dream of the opportunity to own their own homes."

Habitat believes in the opportunity for home ownership, and in New York City the organization is finding innovative ways to create that opportunity in a city that has nowhere to expand. One recent project is an affordable housing development with fifty-seven units in the Bronx, housing the largest number of families in a single structure in Habitat's history.

Habitat has a long history of disaster relief response in addition to creating housing opportunities, and one of the things Karen is proudest of is the ways in which Habitat has mobilized post-disaster to provide housing solutions to the most vulnerable communities in the aftermath of hurricanes, tsunamis, and earthquakes. Following the catastrophic Asian tsunami in 2004 and Hurricane Katrina in 2005, the organization was forced to look at how they responded in the aftermath of disasters.

"We had to ask ourselves," Karen says, "how do we better address the housing post-disaster?" Historically, housing solutions came much later, after the Red Cross and other aid agencies came in to provide initial response and relief to those most affected.

Habitat developed a "pathways to partnership" model to address how to help families rebuild more quickly. "We developed strategies that go into place right after the disaster, including a shelter kit that allows populations to have shelter in place immediately." This has provided the poorest populations with tools to shelter in place. "After a disaster there is so much chaos, and these kits and more formalized transitional shelters not only help people right away, but can be moved if needed."

Habitat has also piloted other innovative shelter delivery solutions, including post-Katrina, with a program called House in a Box, Karen explains. Volunteers framed small homes outside of public arenas, such as baseball stadiums, and even in Rockefeller Plaza, to promote the importance and urgency of shelter. This gave people the opportunity to be of service to the suffering communities, even from afar. Materials were then stacked and packed to be shipped and reassembled in their permanent locations in disaster-impacted zones. "While Habitat for Humanity's focus is always on affordable home ownership, we also seek to provide housing solutions to as many vulnerable communities as possible," Karen tells me.

As our interview comes to an end, Karen stands to point out a photograph of President Jimmy Carter hugging Garth Brooks, both of whom are deeply involved in the organization. "This was such a moving moment," she shares, "during a project following the devastating earthquakes in Haiti."

Her role in Habitat has brought her into contact with some of the most vulnerable populations in the world, and some of the highest-profile celebrities of our times. She laughs when recalling that she ended up feeling more like Mary Tyler Moore through Habitat for Humanity, than through her work in television, when she worked alongside *The Today Show* staff building the Houses in a Box in Rockefeller Plaza, and was given an executive pass to the newsroom.

Ultimately, she says, the best part of the work is the realization that we're more alike than we are different. With her eyes still lingering on the framed image of Carter and Brooks, she says, "Doing this type of work makes me feel more a part of the world than separate from it."

photo © Lieutenant Governor's Office

KATHY HOCHUL,
NYS LIEUTENANT GOVERNOR

"Women often transcend party politics."

—KATHY HOCHUL, lieutenant governor, New York State

I arrived for my interview with New York State Lieutenant Governor Kathy Hochul in New York City on the coldest day recorded in the city this year, December 18, 2019. As I was escorted by one of her aides to her office, I commented about what a pleasure it was to step into such a warm room given the chill outside.

"I can guarantee women's offices will be warmer," Kathy replied with a chuckle.

Once we sat down for the interview, Kathy had much more to say about the many benefits women leaders bring to political office. "Women are more apt to reach out across party lines to find common ground and common causes," she continued. "I think that is the strength of women in leadership at every level."

Citing one example, Kathy recalled when she was first elected to the US House of Representatives in June 2011, representing New York's 26th Congressional District. "That got me to Washington," she said, "but I had nowhere to stay." Congresswoman Carolyn Maloney immediately reached out to ask her where she would be living. When Kathy replied that she hadn't yet figured out a place, Carolyn invited her to stay at her home.

"She felt a sisterhood with me because people had also told her she couldn't win," said Kathy, who was told she wouldn't win a congressional seat since she had no name recognition and was running as a Democrat in one of the most Republican districts.

When Debbie Wasserman Schultz, then chair of the Democratic National Committee, greeted Kathy in Washington, her first question to her was, "Can you play softball?" Kathy thought for a moment before responding. The real answer was that she couldn't, but she also hadn't run for Congress before. So she said, "Yes, I can play, of course."

On her next trip home, Kathy asked her husband to teach her how to throw, catch, and swing a bat. When she returned to Washington, DC, she started to practice with the other players on the team regularly at seven thirty in the morning. "We practiced on a rundown ballfield, whereas the male members of Congress practiced in a professional stadium," she said.

I told Kathy that her baseball experience mirrored one I had when I played on a girls' Little League team, although it was forty years earlier. I played in the Lassie League, where there were four teams mildly named the Bunnies, the Chicks, the Pixies, and the Kittens. It was 1971, and the Lassie League played on an old field with no scoreboard. We weren't given full uniforms like the boys' teams, just T-shirts with the team name and number on the back. We also couldn't wear cleats, although the boys did.

"One day," I told Kathy, "the boys' teams forfeited their game, which was scheduled to be played on the better field, so we were invited to play there that day. It had newer grounds, an electronic scoreboard, and a staff who announced each player's name as they stepped up to the plate."

I recalled feeling ecstatic over this turn of events—that even for just one game, our team would get to experience what the boys' teams always got. But then, as our team walked over to the newer field, our excitement turned to disappointment as the staff suddenly left. "At least they didn't roll up the field and take that along with them too." Kathy reacted with a knowing laugh.

The fact that forty years later, women players—and members of Congress at that—were still being relegated to poorer playing conditions seemed horrifying. But then Kathy explained why the congressional softball games were meaningful. "We all practiced on that old field together, Democratic and Republican women in the House and the Senate," she said, smiling brightly. "Politics were put aside as we all engaged in a team effort."

Their first game was played against members of the media. "Senator Kirsten Gillibrand was the pitcher, Debbie Wasserman Schultz was the shortstop, and I played center field—I think that was because I'm a Democrat in the most Republican district in the state," she said with a laugh. While the average age of congressional players was fifty-three, the average age of the players on the media team was twenty-seven. Still, the congressional team won.

"I was so new to playing softball that when I got my first hit, I plowed into the player on first base. I didn't know you're not supposed to do that," Kathy said with a laugh. But the second time she got a hit, she did the same thing. "I showed the other team that they weren't going to get in my way," she said. After her team won, they went to a dive bar. She remembered that someone chose Neil Diamond's "Sweet Caroline" on the jukebox. "I got to be friends with all of these Republican women, which is so uncommon because rarely anyone crosses the aisle to befriend a member of the other party." She explained how the men's experience is so different because the teams are separated by political party, Democrats against Republicans. "And they play against each other with a vengeance," she said. "It's a shame. There's no collaboration or sense of community. Such a lost opportunity for them."

On the day I interviewed Kathy, she was dressed all in purple, since she would be giving a speech following our meeting in support of janitors demanding fairer contracts from their union. Their official color is purple. Kathy sat behind her large brown wood desk, her large green eyes gleaming, offset by her shoulder-length auburn hair. Hanging on the wall behind her was a large poster displaying a breathtaking view of Niagara Falls, with the words NEW YORK STATE boldly printed just below it, and I LOVE NY just below that. Behind her to her right stood the American flag, and on the wood cabinet to her left lay a yellow sash with the word WOMEN emblazoned on it in bold letters.

The centerpiece of her office was a floor-to-ceiling bookcase standing against the long horizontal wall to the left of her desk. I noticed a number of items that paid tribute to her commitments and accomplishments in political office: volumes of the United States Code of Law stood alongside the plaques, proclamations, and glass trophies. I also noticed a white hardhat with the words "LGBT Network" printed across the front, and a rainbow teddy bear from World Pride NYC in 2019, both testaments to Kathy's commitment to the LGBTQ community. As lieutenant governor, she presided over the passage of GENDA, the Gender Expression Non-Discrimination Act, and legislation protecting LGBTQ youth from conversion therapy.

How Kathy rose to become the lieutenant governor of New York State and the first Democratic woman to serve two terms in this position had to do with her determination, but there was also calculated risk involved. Her early career was rooted in advocating for women and girls, joining her mother and aunt in establishing the Kathleen Mary House, a transitional home for victims of domestic violence located in Blasdell, New York, in 2006.

From 2007 to 2011, she served as Erie County clerk, but

when it came to her next political campaign, she was at a cross-roads. "I remember thinking that I could run again for county clerk in Erie County, and I thought I could easily win, or I could run for a seat in Congress and be very likely to lose," she recalled. At the time, she had no name recognition, and she'd be running for a congressional seat as a Democrat in one of the most Republican districts in New York. "I spoke with my family about it and laid out the pros and cons," she continued. But it was her twenty-one-year-old daughter, Katie, who convinced her to run for Congress. "You have to," Kathy recalled she said. "I then knew I had to show her that her mother had the guts to do something others thought was impossible. It was a lesson for her, and for me."

Kathy won the election, in part, due to her unyielding defense of Medicare and Social Security. During her campaign, Paul Ryan was trying to end both of these programs, which provide free federal insurance programs for people aged sixty-five and older. Kathy defended these two programs nationally and received the endorsement of a number of women's groups, including Emily's List. "I was able to zero in and nationalize this issue, which also enabled me to win over Republican senior women in the district," Kathy recalls. "I spoke with them about this common issue that transcended party politics, and despite millions of dollars spent by the Koch Brothers and Karl Rove on advertisements meant to demonize me, I won. I had no right to win this district politically," she continued, "but it stopped many Republicans in their tracks. People have a right to healthcare."

Just ten days before our interview, Kathy had been elected chair of the Democratic Lieutenant Governors Association (DLGA), an organization focused on electing Democratic Lieutenant Governors nationally each year. "As dysfunction continues to stall Washington, more responsibility is falling on governors and lieutenant governors to fill the serious void of leadership and continue to set the example of government working for the people—from confronting climate change to job creation to supporting women and working families," Kathy wrote in her announcement.

Before our interview was over, I asked her whether there was any particular message or story she wanted to share with me.

"Yes," she said. "I was walking through the Nine Eleven Museum yesterday, and it harkened to a time when our sense of humanity and common interests were powerful. We have to get back to this, but without experiencing another disaster of epic proportions. We need to put aside the destructive divisiveness in our country today. Also," she continued, "We need to address why women don't run for office in the first place."

She spoke with me for a while about how women lack confidence, believing that they have to be "110 percent qualified" before even running. She lamented this reality and shared how this had been true for her too. "I was that woman who didn't have confidence. I didn't think I was qualified enough to run, even though I worked as an activist in college, became an attorney, and worked for Democratic candidates locally. I always felt I needed to wait until I was more qualified to run for even the lowest rung in government."

She then told me a story of a twenty-two-year-old man who had just graduated from college and still lived with his parents when he decided to run for a position on her local town board. "That was my wake-up call," she said. "I thought to myself, I have more experience than this twenty-two-year-old." She grinned at me. Her children were preschoolers at the time, and she took them along with her while knocking on people's doors. As it turned out, two seats opened on the town board, and she and the twenty-two-year-old won them. Looking back, she said, "The person who was wrong was me. He had a lot of confidence in himself at such a young age. He made success happen for himself. To think I almost didn't run."

Her hope is to see more young women run for office because,

she said, "When they run, they often win." Kathy hopes that by telling her own story she can help them along. "Only in the past few years have I developed the confidence to be a leader," she told me. "I'd like to cut that short for younger women by telling them they don't have to wait. The guys don't. Women should think the same way. We need women's voices." With that, she rose to her feet and picked up a clipped set of pages from her desk, which included her upcoming speech to the janitors' union. Her final words to me conveyed the message that had been the through thread of the entire interview: "We need diversity at the table."

JESSICA HOUSSIAN

*"It is with deep humility that I admit to
not having all of the answers."*

—JESSICA HOUSSIAN, cofounder and co-CEO,
Equality Fund

"This is a feminist home," Jessica told me when I first walked into her swank apartment in Manhattan's SoHo, a neighborhood lauded for its chic fashion boutiques and celebrated artists' lofts and galleries. Jessica's apartment feels welcoming. Looking around, I noted a number of paintings of women posed in graceful positions hanging on the exposed brick walls just above couches and chairs wrapped in soft ivories, offset by the industrial and retro-looking kitchen appliances and countertops basking in steel metal finishes above the dark hardwood floors. Jessica was quick to point out that all the paintings were by female artists. But it is behind those walls where feminism more strongly resides.

"When this apartment was under construction, I snuck in with a friend and wrote feminist quotes all over the walls—from Audre Lorde, ("Revolution is not a one-time event.") to Gloria Steinem ("The truth will set you free. But first it will piss you off."). And they're still there, under the drywall, inspiring me every minute I spend here," she told me, her eyes scanning the perimeter of the apartment. She laughs as she recalls the remodeling process, and how her contractor called her one day to say that somebody had broken in and written all over the walls.

"Read the quotes," she laughed, and I can see that she's deep in a nostalgic moment. For Jessica, New York City is her second home. Her first is Vancouver, British Columbia, where her family still resides. She chose New York in her twenties, after visiting here for the first time in 1996. "When I first came to New York City, I immediately identified with the John Updike quote that says, 'The true New Yorker secretly believes that people living anywhere else have to be, in some sense, kidding.'" She sat forward, self-assuredly.

The first time I met Jessica was a couple of weeks before this interview. I received an email from the Equality Fund's communications lead requesting an interview and follow-up article in Women's eNews about the Equality Fund, an organization Jessica cofounded. I immediately agreed. I had only recently learned about this fund at the Women Deliver Summit, a global conference that had taken place in Vancouver a few weeks earlier in June 2019. We'd both attended the four-day conference.

On June 4, the second day of the conference, I waited inside a secured briefing room, along with a few dozen other journalists, for the arrival of Canadian Prime Minister Justin Trudeau. He was there to make a major announcement about his country's commitment to supporting the health of women and girls around the world. Although his speech lasted no more than twenty minutes, it did not disappoint. Announcing that the Government of Canada would raise its funding beginning in 2023 to reach $1.4

billion annually in support of sexual and reproductive health rights and maternal, newborn, and child health, this commitment would also ensure that $600 million of the annual investment will be dedicated to ensuring women have the right to make their own decisions about their bodies.

The Equality Fund would be one of the primary beneficiaries of these efforts, having been granted $300 million to develop a funding platform for women's rights organizations in developing countries.

Jessica agreed to meet with me right away, at a restaurant near my office on the Upper West Side of Manhattan. She's in her thirties, and had already established herself as a powerful force for women and girls as a current board member of the Canadian Women's Foundation, and the former executive director of Women Moving Millions, a nonprofit organization based in the US that brings powerful philanthropists together to fund efforts establishing gender equality throughout the world, particularly where the widest gaps exist. Jessica's knowledge was sweeping, her focus unwavering, her warmth all-embracing.

When we sat down, I told Jessica that the last time I was at this restaurant had been six months earlier, just before my little dog had passed away at the age of fourteen. Tears immediately welled in her eyes. "I have a little dog as well, Eloise," she said. "She's thirteen." I was surprised by the level of openness she displayed so quickly and easily, particularly with someone she just met, and asked her about it. "Vulnerability is a critical component of leadership," she said to me, leaning forward, her eyes focused directly on me. "The past few years have been an evolution for me," she continued. "I feel like I've been on a steep learning journey about myself—to venture outside of what feels like a safe zone of comfort, and that is where growth happens." She then mentioned the type of leadership made famous by Brené Brown, who teaches about the importance of leaders being "all in," even though they may fail. "It is all about stepping into uncertainty and emotional exposure," Jessica added. "This shows true courage."

Our meeting ended after an hour, both of us having to rush to another appointment, and when I asked her if I might interview her for my book, she readily agreed that we could get together for a follow-up meeting at her home a few weeks later.

As I rode up the elevator to her fourth-floor apartment the following month, I was immediately struck by the words ELOISE LIVES HERE in brass letters on the front door. I smiled, recalling her tearful reaction to the news of my losing my dog. *Of course these are the words that would welcome Jessica's visitors,* I thought.

Greeting me with a warm hug, she invited me into the kitchen where she poured me a glass of sparkling water. "I remembered this is what you like," she said, since that was what I'd ordered at the restaurant at our first meeting.

She walked me over to the rectangular wooden dining room table and told me she couldn't believe I wanted her to be in my book.

"I used to turn down so many invitations, uncomfortable about emerging as a leader in this field. I was saying 'no' a lot," she said, her eyes cast downward. "But then I decided to embark on a year of 'yes,' saying 'yes' to everything that came my way." She looked up at me, her eyes appearing even more determined. "It pushed me out of my comfort zone. I had a wild year, speaking publicly and accepting invitations to join numerous boards." That was in 2014, which she now described as a "tipping point" in her career. Although she no longer accepts every invitation, it was a great way for her to step into her confidence. "Since then," she said with a wide grin, "it has turned into years of 'possibly.'"

Still, as a woman, and especially one who's under forty, she often feels the pressure to be excellent all the time. "I'm aware of the doubt that sometimes exists when I walk into a room full of older men," she told me. "But, to quote Audre Lorde, 'When I dare to be powerful and use my strengths in the service of my vision, that becomes less and less important, and I'm no longer afraid.'" I could see in that moment how she must appear in front of a room of her elders—confident, charismatic, passionate. She quoted Audre Lorde again: "'I speak for those women who do not have a voice because they are so terrified. We've been taught that silence will save us, but it won't.'"

This is the very premise upon which the Equality Fund was born. The brainchild of Jessica and two other feminists, Jess Tomlin and Sophie Gupta, the Equality Fund came about, Jessica recalled, when "we wondered what it would look like if a country like Canada, which currently has feminist leadership, would make a big bet on women's rights and codesign a totally new and innovative model for its people, where women and girls are a priority." From that, the Fund responded to the Canadian government's invitation for a proposal, as one of several bidders. Of all that moved forward to the next round, the Equality Fund came out on top.

Yet, this unprecedented funding award represents only a portion of the fund's larger goal, which is to mobilize over a billion dollars for gender equality. They aim to disrupt traditional funding mechanisms through a feminist approach based upon three core themes: shifting power, building peace, and protecting the planet. All of this is striving toward the goal of a gender-equal world. Still, Jessica described the Equality Fund's role as only "midwives of the goal, not the mothers of it."

"It is something that belongs to Canada," she told me, "and it's my hope that it has a legacy for the future of this country."

Already, Jessica said she is witnessing how collaborative this model is. "People from different sectors, including technology, venture capital, and other large corporations, are working together unlike they have ever before. They're learning how to speak 'feminist,' and we're learning how to speak 'banker.'"

Yet, it's not only major corporations with significant resources that have shown their support. "Beatrice, my seven-year-old niece, held a bake sale at her school in Vancouver. And our first donors were eleven-year-old girls who handed me $230 in a mason jar from selling cookies," Jessica said proudly. "They said they understood what I was trying to do, and they wanted to be part of it."

She told me that one of the conversations she often has with her cofounders is about the right time to transition, or to "hand off the baton," as she calls it. "I feel privileged to be building this, but I also love the idea of being very intentional," she told me. "There will be a time when the fund is handed over to the next leaders, where they can take it to a place that I never could. That's what I hope for."

Toward the end of our interview, Jessica told me that she strives to surround herself with people whom she calls "the cleverest leaders," those who have even better ideas that she does. "I am only happy when I put other people in a room who are smarter than I am," she said, smiling again. "I'm always aware of my place in the ecosystem, and I believe that for the long-term viability and sustainability of my work to continue, I must build from the top up, rather than from the top down."

SWANEE HUNT

"Women will do everything they can to prevent war."

—SWANEE HUNT, author, activist and
former US ambassador to Austria (1993–1997)

The first time I walked into Swanee Hunt's Washington, DC, home in May 2019, I felt like I was standing in a museum. Sculptures, paintings, and illustrations of various kinds were scattered throughout her home. A silk tapestry made from Indian wedding dresses hung on the wall alongside a proclamation naming Swanee ambassador to Austria signed by then President William Jefferson Clinton.

I traveled there from New York City to attend a symposium on the status of human trafficking in the US. As the founder and chair of Demand Abolition, an activist organization committed to eradicating the illegal commercial sex industry, Hunt had sponsored the event. "The solution to end sex trafficking is to end sex buying," Swanee told the audience as she stood at the podium. "Men who buy sex create the demand that fuels the illegal sex trade. Without buyers, prostitution and sex trafficking would cease to exist."

Her goal to end the illegal sex trade is an arduous one, but advancing feminism in the US and around the world is Swanee's calling. From 1993 to 1997, when she served as ambassador to Austria, she hosted negotiations and international symposia and met with grassroots women leaders to help establish peace in the neighboring Balkan states. As the founder of the Women and Public Policy Program at Harvard Kennedy School, she urged present and future leaders to create a more gender-equal world. Swanee consults with government officials and civil society leaders across the globe. She is most known for her work in increasing the participation and inclusion of women in peace processes around the world.

She greeted me at the door wearing casual, loose-fitting black pants with a matching shirt. She was barefoot. As I followed her through the long walkway to the kitchen, she introduced me to her two home companions, a spoiled snow-white cat named Zhivago and a small green parrot with a yellow beak named Mellow. "His name is very appropriate; he calms me," she said as she fed him peanut butter with a tiny spoon. "It's his favorite food," she added, shooting me a grin. Swanee has been very much the gracious hostess on two occasions, and on this visit, like the last one, she invited me to stay overnight in her guest room.

Her passion to create social change is reflected in her extensive writing, mostly on the topic of gender. Some of her many commentaries have been published in Women's eNews, including her September 2009 article, "She Speaks Serious Change, Carries Big Purse," in which she explained how her determination to right society's wrongs first developed.

She wrote, "When you grow up as I did with a father zealously committed to political change, it gets into your blood." Swanee's father, a famously conservative Texas oil tycoon, passed away when she was only twenty-four years old, but she carried on his passion for activism even as she made a hard left turn politically. She went on to write about how, in 1979, when she made a reservation for a table in the male-only main dining room of the

Dallas Petroleum Club, no one knew she was a woman because of her first name. "When I arrived, the stately but flummoxed black maître d' had to turn me away or lose his job. He and I had more in common than met the eye: Neither of us was welcome in the hallowed mess hall where deals might be made."

In a March 2018 Women's eNews article, "The Women, Peace, and Security Act: A Rare Milestone," she described one of the "few hopeful moments in American politics that year." "Passage of the Women, Peace, and Security Act was a quiet bipartisan landmark, the culmination of more than two decades of relentless advocacy to involve women in decisions on war and peace. But it was also just a first step toward turning this lofty goal into daily practice for the US government and its many agencies that deal with peace and security," she warned.

In 2001, she authored "Rwandan Women Dying from Genocide's Legacy of AIDS," which explored and demystified the toll AIDS had taken over the previous twenty years, and predictions of the epidemic's consequences, including real-life stories. "I met with women whose destinies were forever marked by the violence," she wrote. "Among them was Solange, who was only eight years old when the militia kidnapped her. She and four other girls were kept for three weeks and raped repeatedly, each day. At the end, only two were alive. Upon her return home, she began to get sick. At the hospital, she received a death sentence: HIV. That's a death sentence shared by many African women who were raped in the course of other brutal conflicts throughout the continent." HIV AIDS is no longer a death sentence, but it was very real at the time.

Swanee has told the stories of many Rwandan women and their experiences, particularly about how some of them transformed their lives after the country's hundred-day genocide in 1994.

In her 2017 book, *Rwandan Women Rising*, Swanee wrote of their successful transformation of their country, ultimately creating a parliament where women comprised 64 percent. She shared the stories of seventy women, revealing their immeasurable losses as well as the boundless challenges they experienced in working to rebuild their country, which they ultimately did. Former President Jimmy Carter wrote in the book's foreword: "These women's accomplishments provide important lessons for policy makers and activists who are working toward equality elsewhere in Africa and other post-conflict societies. Their stories, told in their own words via interviews woven throughout the book, demonstrate that the best way to reduce suffering and to prevent and end conflicts is to elevate the status of women throughout the world."

Swanee then lifted a book off the living room table. It was one of her own: *This Was Not Our War: Bosnian Women Reclaiming the Peace*, which she wrote in 2004. "While Rwanda was the greatest success, Bosnia was the greatest failure," she said. In her book, she draws upon seven years of interviews in the 1990s to write about the experiences of twenty-six Bosnian women, each working to reconstruct their country after years of devastation from war. These included stories of a professor who survived the Holocaust, a college student resettling refugees, a businesswoman running nonprofit organizations, and many others. In each case, the women used their survival skills to rebuild a society which they agreed had been destroyed by political greed, and Swanee memorialized their stories. In contrast to Rwanda, the women of Bosnia were overlooked by policy makers charged with forging peace. Swanee says it's not surprising that Bosnia, though no longer actively at war, remains a tinderbox.

As we moved into her living room to sit in front of the fireplace, Swanee asked me if I knew the term "soft power," coined by Joseph Nye, former Dean of the Harvard Kennedy School of Government. She explained his concept, in which orders are not just handed down by a leader who is "king of the mountain," but instead where visions are conveyed, emotional intelligence is used to reach out to others, and nonverbal communication is considered as important as verbal skills. "Without soft power," Swanee told me, "we miss out on a crucial way to lead effectively."

In her preface to *This Was Not Our War,* Swanee observed that in Bosnia—and she said this was true of war in general—"those who waged the war were selected to plan and implement the peace, a ludicrous tradition rarely questioned by otherwise enlightened leaders in the foreign policy establishment." This book's foreword was also written by a former US president, this time Bill Clinton. He wrote: "Replacing tyranny with justice, healing deep scars, exchanging hatred for hope . . . the women in *This Was Not Our War* teach us how."

Swanee then closed the book, laid it back down on the table, and looked up at me. "People say that war is good for the economy? It fails the economy. Too often profits go to wealthy people building yachts instead of building schools. We need to know where the money is circulating. It is either circulating in ways that are positive or destructive. While some progressive countries are using money to ensure one hundred percent of its citizens are going to school instead of prison, the US has the highest incarceration rate in the world."

Before our interview came to an end, I asked Swanee if there was anything else she wanted to make sure I included in my book.

"Yes," she said. "What I am now working on most is my program Demand Abolition, whose purpose is to eliminate the purchasing of illegal commercial sex. I decided to approach the end of sex trafficking not by rescuing women and girls, but by going upstream from the problem, to end the demand. Research indicates that eighty-six percent of men who buy sex say they would stop if a family member were to find out." She cited Sweden's practice of sending postcards to arrested sex buyers' homes showing a date for them to appear in court. This often enables a family member to see the card first.

She then laughed, saying, "I think we should use turquoise paper, so the card really stands out." Swanee wants to see extensive training of US law enforcement to arrest the male buyers and not the girls and women in the sex trade, most of whom aren't there of their own free will and are victims of sexual and other heinous violence. "The police now conduct a stakeout of a hotel room where they see the trafficked girl being brought into the room," she said, "and watch as the buyers come in and out of the room, but they are not arrested. In too many cases, they arrest the victim, not the real perpetrator. I think the male police officers often identify with the guys, unfortunately."

Swanee closed our interview on this note: "Who is going to do this work if I don't? I am fortunate to have the wealth, the education, and the connections to make a difference."

Swanee again opened her book on Bosnia to write a personal note to me inside. She handed it to me, and I placed in my briefcase alongside her book on Rwanda, which she had given me a year earlier. I then opened Rwandan Women Rising, and turned to my favorite quote in the book. "But after this interview," I told Swanee as I pointed to it, "It holds even more meaning":

Women understand most the importance of peace.
In conflicts, women are the ones hurt most,
so each will participate in the recovery some way.
Look at the key institutions in our country today.
Women are providing leadership.
There's no way you can talk about the transformation
of society unless that group is involved.
Much as we want to benefit from this process,
we also want to be a part of it.
There's no way you can avoid 55 percent of a
population and think they'll be just recipients.
We have to be agents of peace.

We can't just have peace delivered to us on a plate.

—ALOISEA INYUMBA, Rwanda's minister for gender
and family promotion (1964–2012)

photo © The Edna Adan University Hospital

EDNA ADAN ISMAIL

"I am a woman, the mother of the nation, and a nurse."
"I have been fighting for women's rights forever."
"I was born into this."

—EDNA ADAN ISMAIL, director/founder,
the Edna Adan University Hospital

It is my favorite conference of the year, the Women in the World Summit, where women from around the world gather in New York City each April to break the silence surrounding censorship, patriarchy, and injustice; where women share stories, inspire change, and awaken the next generation of female leaders. Celebrating its tenth anniversary in 2019, the summit attracted such well-known speakers as Hillary Clinton, Oprah Winfrey, and Anna Wintour. Yet, there was one woman who, although not nearly as famous, has done more to improve the lives of women than almost any of the others.

It was by pure luck that I was seated at the same table as Edna Adan Ismail at the summit's dinner at New York City's

Time Warner Center building. While a variety of conversations flowed among those seated at my table, there was one discussion I overheard that particularly caught my attention. Edna Adan Ismail was sitting just two seats to my right; the executive director of her foundation sat between us. A number of attendees from other tables walked over to Edna over the course of the dinner, introducing themselves while shaking her hand in respect. I did not know who Edna was, although clearly dressed in her native clothing, including a multicolored headscarf that covered all her hair and wrapped tightly around her face, as well as a matching long and loose-fitting dress, I suspected she was from Africa.

"Somaliland," she replied, after I inquired. "Not Somalia, as our country is sometimes mistaken for. Somaliland," she emphasized. I then overheard her tell a story to another dinner guest about how she has had to step in to save the lives of women during childbirth by convincing their husbands to sign a form approving life-saving Caesarian sections. "If they did not sign, I then turned the form over and drew a line," she said, while demonstrating an imaginary line being drawn with her index finger. "So I say to them, 'Then sign here instead,' alongside the words where I write, 'I want my wife to die,'" she recounted. "After reading that, the husband signs for his wife's surgery every single time," she said, smiling proudly. Upon overhearing this story of daring and courage, I asked her colleague if we could schedule a time for me to interview her. She responded the next day and scheduled an interview before Edna was to fly back to her country one week later.

"I am just doing what needs to be done," Edna said at the beginning of our interview at New York's High Line Hotel just a few days later. In the hotel's lobby, there were many guests sitting around us, talking on their cell phones and typing on their computers, but Edna easily held my attention with her strong and empowering presence. The hotel's lobby, sporting its original 1895 Gothic design capturing both magnificent height and grace, actually served as an ideal setting to meet Edna, reflecting the grace she similarly embodied. Dressed in a brown-and-white headscarf and matching long dress, similar in fabric and length to her attire when I first met her a few days earlier, her face reflected the strength of her convictions, while exuding radiance and warmth. Her eyes were dark and deep, genial and focused. Her beaming white smile was uncompromising.

Often described as the Muslim Mother Teresa, Edna has held a number of diplomatic roles in her native country of Somaliland, including foreign minister, minister of family welfare and development, and first lady. Yet, despite her powerful political roles, she is perhaps best known for the hospital she built in her name, after selling most of her possessions in 2002.

Unlike the majority of the feminist leaders I've interviewed for this book, however, Edna did not initially develop her altruistic qualities of compassion, generosity, and devotion from other women. Rather, she learned them at a very early age from her father, a prominent physician. "When I was a child, the problems of the world came to my father's door," Edna recalled with pride. "His patients came before his own needs." Witnessing his selflessness on a daily basis, she had the unique experience of internalizing these qualities from a male figure who was instrumental in her life. "I was born into this," she said, "and what I learned from my father, I brought into my diplomatic career."

One of five siblings (two of whom died during childbirth), Edna was born in 1937, a time when girls were not permitted to be educated in Somaliland. When her father hired a tutor to teach some local boys, however, he also encouraged her to learn to read and write along with them. Later, she attended school in Djibouti where her aunt was a teacher, and this education eventually led Edna to become the first Somaliland girl to study in Britain. "My father always believed that I should not have any educational limits in my life," Edna recalled. Yet, she still had to undergo numerous battles to reach her full learning potential, since Somaliland's education system was strictly patriarchal. Even after becoming the first Somaliland woman to earn an education in Britain and return to her homeland as its first qualified nurse, it took almost two years before the state paid her for her work in one of its hospitals. Further, despite learning to drive a car while in Britain, she struggled for years to get her driver's license in Somaliland. Eventually she became the country's first woman to do so.

Yet her progressive upbringing did not prevent her from undergoing one of her country's most long-held and barbaric customs. When Edna was just eight years old, her mother and grandmother arranged for her to undergo female genital mutilation (FGM) while her father was away on a business trip. "When my father returned home, he was furious," Edna recalled. "He didn't believe in this custom; not at all." It was due to her determination to prevent other girls from undergoing the same trauma that she went on to train as a nurse and midwife in the United Kingdom at the Borough Polytechnic, now London South Bank University.

"The fight against FGM has been the biggest battle of my life—and every moment of my life has been a battle," Edna continued. "Girls in my country survived everything from the measles to whooping cough to diarrhea, and then at the age of seven or eight, when they are learning to jump, to run, and to speak for themselves, this is done to them." While the history of this ritual practice is unclear, it is most prevalent in cultures that are mainly patriarchal—and it's a dangerous reflection of long-held beliefs supporting gender inequality. Not only can this practice lead to severe pain, excessive bleeding, shock, infections, HIV, and even death, its survivors can also suffer long-term psychological effects such as post-traumatic stress disorder. One of Edna's goals, therefore, is for fathers to be educated about the dangers of FGM, to hopefully encourage them to protect their daughters. To do so, she is now working on publishing an animated book about its dangers, since so many adults in her country cannot read. "It's not only cutting, it's total mutilation!" she asserted.

As the director and founder of the Edna Adan University Hospital in Hargeisa, Edna's mission is to help improve the health of the local inhabitants and, even more urgently, to decrease Somaliland's extreme levels of maternal and infant mortality, which are among the highest in the world. This nonprofit teaching hospital, which Edna had built from scratch, is also training student nurses and other health professionals. "Somaliland now has the largest per capita of midwives throughout the world," she told me proudly.

Officially opened on March 9, 2002, the hospital was built on land donated to her by the local government at a site formerly used as a garbage dump. The region lacked trained midwives and nurses, as most had either fled the country or been killed during the Somali Civil War (1998–1999), which destroyed Somaliland's entire health infrastructure. Edna recruited more than thirty candidates and began training them while the hospital was still under construction. "Even while training these women, I had to help them build their own character and lead their own lives. Often, at the beginning of training, they appeared so scared and so small—even at the age of eighteen years old," Edna reflected. "When I would ask them their names, for example, they would respond in a whisper while looking down at their shoes," Edna lamented. "I would then tell them, 'Look up at me when you answer. I am more important than your shoes. Don't be invisible.'" Through ongoing training at Edna's hospital, many of these women have since become surgeons. "When I see them running through the halls of my hospital during medical emergencies, I proudly say to myself, I trained you so that you can save that woman's life."

Today the hospital houses two operating rooms, a laboratory, a library, a computer center, and a university dedicated to training nurses and midwives, as well as other health professionals.

As of 2018, it has grown to two hundred staff members and fifteen hundred students. "Due to our training, our country has been able to reduce infant mortality significantly," Edna said. This facility is also Edna's home; she first moved in when the hospital was still under construction.

Further, as Somaliland's first woman minister of social affairs (August 2002–June 2003), and then its foreign minister, she found she was able to more powerfully present the case for supporting Somaliland, not only as a diplomat, but as a woman, to leaders of other countries.

"Because I am a woman," Edna told me, "I can share emotions I feel by witnessing the pain and injustice my country has suffered." Today, as the former foreign minister of Somaliland, she hosts numerous delegations at the hospital. "I do this so that I can prove to everyone that if this site is good enough for my patients and also good enough for me to live in, then it is good enough for those who wish to associate with me." As the only woman in the international delegation of foreign ministers, she often has to remind other dignitaries that she serves as its head. "If I bang on a table or shed a tear, don't try to appease me, I tell them. When I express anger, don't tell me to cool down," she continued. "Don't try to impose a different emotion from what I am expressing at that moment. I will know when I want to cool down, and I will tell you what I need. If I wish to show my emotions, it is because I have chosen to do so."

Edna's accomplishments are enormous, and yet she's still not nearly finished. "I want to get my country internationally recognized," she told me. "That is my unfinished book." She glanced at the floor for a moment before looking back up at me, even more intently. "The world is ignoring the presence of a democratic country in Somaliland. We have managed to demobilize our militia with our own resources; we have a functioning democratically elected government, and we generate all taxes from our own country. While the international community is spending billions of dollars to try to bring peace in Somalia, they are ignoring the peace we have already achieved in Somaliland. We gain from peace and stability. They gain from lawlessness."

And with that, Edna rose to her feet and gave me an embracing hug as I left our interview. Before I exited the hotel lobby, I looked back one last time, and noticed that her eyes were still fixed on me, displaying all of the compassion and courage it took for her to get here.

KATJA IVERSEN

*"Once we break old gender norms, men will
also be able to better live their full lives."*

—KATJA IVERSEN, president and CEO, Women Deliver

We bonded over Pippi Longstocking, the fictional red-haired and freckled nine-year-old girl from the 1950s children's book series. I, as a child in New York City, and Katja, some four thousand miles away in Denmark, both identified with her and admired her independence (she lived on her own with only a pet monkey and horse as companions) and her heroic ability to handle all challenges she encountered, including protecting other children from bullies. "She is the 'strongest girl in the world,'" Katja said to me with a wide smile, recalling Pippi's repeated self-proclamation throughout the four-book series, which has been translated into 40 languages, has sold 165 million copies worldwide, and has also been made into a television series and a film.

I nodded. "Yes, she is!"

It was January 2019 when Katja and I met at Women Deliver's headquarters in Manhattan's SoHo neighborhood. I requested an interview with her as a potential honoree for Women's eNews's 21 Leaders for the 21st Century 2019 awards. Under Katja's leadership as president and CEO since 2014, Women Deliver had grown from a staff of eleven to sixty. As I stepped into the company's office space on the ninth floor of a historic building in SoHo, I was greeted by a wide open and brightly lit space, devoid of any dividing walls between desks, creating a feeling of complete openness and community. Only a few private meeting rooms encased in glass walls were interspersed, each named after a city where important international gender agreements had been made—or where the big triennial Women Deliver conference had been held. My interview with Katja took place in the Beijing room, which I mentioned to Katja was quite apropos, since in 1995 the United Nations Fourth World Conference on Women had been held in that city, and that was also where then First Lady Hillary Clinton proclaimed, "Women's rights are human rights."

Katja greeted me with a welcoming handshake, and handed me a pin carrying the Women Deliver's logo, a bright yellow arrow pointing upward and toward you. Its tagline read: "Invest in Girls and Women," and as Katja said, "It points to yourself first, because that is where all change starts."

It became quite clear early on in our interview that Katja would serve as an ideal 21 Leader honoree. She spoke of how gender equality is a "net positive for everybody," and how women's economic empowerment enhances families, communities, and nations. "Gender equality is not just a women's problem. It is a societal issue, and a win-win. If we really want to create an equal world, men have to be involved as well," Katja said. She spoke in a gentle yet confident tone. Her red-framed eyeglasses accentuated her blue eyes, while complementing her blond, shoulder-length hair. There was a gentleness in the way she presented herself, yet she also exuded a calm and steady strength.

Katja then told me that one of the effective ways to establish universal gender norms was by enhancing fathers' connections to their babies. "When paternity leave is considered necessary rather than just a perk, and when childcare—and care work in general—becomes a joint responsibility, traditional gender norms will be broken, and we can move toward a more equal world, where women—and men—can live their full potential." She reiterated this message when she accepted her award that May at the Women's eNews annual awards gala. Everyone stood in applause, men as well as women.

I first learned of Women Deliver's work three years earlier when I attended its 2016 summit in Copenhagen, Denmark. Held once every three years, it is the largest conference on gender equality in the world. I was fascinated by the breadth and depth of the topics and issues covered, as well as the speakers participating, from Melinda Gates of the Bill and Melinda Gates Foundation, to Her Majesty Queen Maxima of the Netherlands, to songwriter and performer Annie Lennox of the British pop music band The Eurythmics. Over six thousand people representing 169 countries, including ministers, parliamentarians, and government representatives from over fifty countries attended, and it was Katja at the helm, opening and closing the summit with bookended speeches that were as disruptive as they were defining. In her reflections of the summit soon afterward, she wrote on the organization's website:

> "The summit provides time and space for us to come together and find commonalities. The international community will never achieve the Sustainable Development Goals or significant progress for girls and women unless we work collaboratively across sectors and issues. Sliced and diced, we are less powerful, our voices weaker."

Just a few weeks after Katja received her award, the next Women Deliver summit was being held, this time in Vancouver, Canada. I attended, and again, the summit did not disappoint in its scope of speakers or number of attendees, which had now reached over eight thousand. Canadian Prime Minister Justin Trudeau chose the summit to announce that the government of Canada would raise its funding to CAD$1.4 billion annually for ten years to support women's and girls' health around the world, which was historically the largest commitment to sexual and reproductive health and rights; President Uhuru Kenyatta of the Republic of Kenya committed to ending female genital mutilation by 2022; and The Global Parliamentary Alliance on Health, Rights, and Development was created, the first ever global platform for parliamentarians to advocate for better health care, expand human rights, and meet the Sustainable Development Goals, both in their home countries and abroad.

Yet, I was most enthralled by two plenary speakers. Neither of them held any titles of political leadership, but their stories were equally heroic, if not more so.

Esenam Nyador made a name for herself as "Miss Taxi," one of the few female taxi drivers in Accra, Ghana, who refused to take no for an answer when she applied to trucking companies for a job as a driver. "When they refused to hire me because I am a woman, they started a war," she said, speaking on stage to over one hundred attendees in the summit's exhibit hall. "I set out from that moment to pump more women into the industry, and I won't stop until there are more women participating in the transport sector," she continued. Wearing blue jeans and a red shirt emblazoned with the words, WE ARE MISS TAXI, Esenam spoke about the business she started, Miss Taxi, for female taxi drivers, as well as the Women Move the City campaign, which trains women to drive city buses. "I want to use my power to give all women the possibility of flying with their talents, grinding gender norms into powder," she said, her smile shining brightly.

Later that day, Nasreen Sheikh, who'd grown up in southern Nepal, stood on one of the other exhibit hall's stages and introduced herself to a crowd of over one hundred at a plenary session. "From the moment of my birth in a southern Nepal border village, I was taught that my existence was unremarkable. Growing up, I witnessed so many atrocities against women that, by age nine or ten, my life seemed destined for the same oppressive path. I worked fifteen hours a day in a Nepali sweatshop as a child laborer, receiving less than two dollars per grueling shift, and only if I completed the hundreds of garments demanded of me. I ate, slept, and toiled in my prison-cell sized sweatshop workstation, too afraid to even look out the window. By age twenty-one, my family had arranged a marriage for me. But through the help of a kind stranger who taught me to read and seize my destiny, I escaped the sweatshop and the forced marriage."

Nasreen would go on to establish a nonprofit organization called Local Women's Handicrafts (LWH), a fair-trade sewing collective based in Kathmandu, Nepal. LWH empowers and educates disadvantaged women by providing a paid training program in design, sewing, weaving, embroidery, knitting, jewelry making, and pattern work. To date, LWH has trained hundreds of Nepali women, many of whom escaped forced and abusive marriages, and all of whom are determined to escape poverty. Following her speech, I walked over to her and told her that I would be publishing an article about her in Women's eNews. After thanking me, she said, "Please also make sure to look at the label on each piece of clothing before you buy it, to make sure it wasn't made overseas in a sweat shop." I promised her I would.

It was not surprising that Katja led such a dynamic organization dedicated to empowering women and girls all over the world, particularly when you consider that, in addition to Pippi Longstocking, she's been inspired by Nelson Mandela as well as her own grandmother.

Three months after the summit, I met with Katja again, this time at her headquarters. She told me about her grandmother first. "It's all my grandmother's fault," she said with a smile, referring to why she chose this as her career. "She was born extremely poor in rural Denmark in 1915," she added. "Her mom was frail and died early, so she had to take care of her four siblings from the age of nothing." She worked as a maid to put her brother through college, and did the same years later for her husband, who became a teacher. But when it was her turn to go to college, it was considered inappropriate for a teacher's wife to work, so she had two children instead.

"And she saved my life when I was born," Katja said, taking a moment's pause to look down at her hands, which were clasped together. "I was born five weeks early, at home with only the midwife, who left an hour later. I was too small to even cry, let alone feed at my mother's breast on my own, so Grandma stepped in, stayed for a month, and made sure we were both okay." As Katja grew older, her grandmother reminded her of the importance of never being financially dependent on a man. "She always told me, 'You're going to get an education, you are going to make your own money, and you're not going to get pregnant before you're ready,'" Katja recalled. "She also lent me money to purchase my first computer—and cried tears of joy when I got the education she never had herself."

Nelson Mandela, whom Katja met a couple of times later in her career, taught Katja to keep fighting for what she believes in, but without bitterness. "He always preached love and collaboration as an ally for gender equality, and for lifting up young people," she told me. "Now, when I speak with people from his cabinet, they tell me that when they doubted they could live up to his expectations and do great things, he not only told them they could do it, but he was also right behind them, supporting them. We need more men and leaders like that."

For Katja, these "teachers" showed her that creating change was possible, but also, that "when you are strong, you have to be kind," as Pippi Longstocking puts it. "They also serve as a reminder that sometimes we have to slow down and ask ourselves if all of our talking and good intentions are actually leading somewhere—to action and concrete results," she cautioned. On that empowered note, Katja rose from her chair, as our meeting was coming to an end, but she made a point to tell me one last thing before we parted ways. "We work hard to change the world, but also have to have a little fun with good partners while we do it."

MARIAM JALABI

"We will not put a gun in any woman's hands."

—MARIAM JALABI, Syrian National Coalition's representative
to the United Nations and founding member of
the Syrian Women's Political Movement

Her six-year-old son's name is Rumi, after the famed thirteenth-century Persian poet renowned for such famously profound quotes as, "Wherever you are, and whatever you do, be in love."

"His philosophy is the religion of all," Mariam told me, explaining why she and her husband chose to name their son after him. "He is a prophet of love, where it doesn't matter what path you come from, as long as you're on the right path," she continued. Mariam is Muslim. Her husband is Jewish.

Mariam lives with her family in Brooklyn, New York. They have two kids, and the younger child is a one-year-old girl named Elmaz, which means "diamond" in Arabic. In addition to speaking English and Arabic at home, they speak Russian. "It's important to know the enemy's language," she said with a grin.

Both Mariam and her husband know what it's like to live among their enemies. Mariam's in-laws were forced to flee Latvia due to persecution of Jews when her husband was just a child. Mariam is the daughter of a doctor who was a member of the nonviolent resistance during the Hafez al-Asaad regime in Syria and was imprisoned five times before the family decided to flee to Germany when Mariam was just five years old. Later, schooled in the Golan Heights, her first chosen career was in the fashion industry, taking her to New York City where she started a company designing clothing for modern Muslim women. "I view clothing as a language through which to liberate women," she told me. In 2011, however, when the Syrian revolution began, her career and her entire life were forever transformed.

I first met Mariam in January 2017 at The John F. Kennedy School of Government at Harvard University. Inclusive Security, a Washington-based nonprofit which consults with global policy-makers on ways to involve women as decision-makers in peace and security processes, was holding its eighteenth annual colloquium. Nine women, each of whom were risking their lives and livelihoods to forge more peaceful paths for their homelands (Kenya, the Philippines, Liberia, Afghanistan, Colombia, Israel, Sri Lanka, Iraq, and Syria), participated in a panel discussion on how to effectively establish peace.

Of all the women on the panel, Mariam stood out. Well-poised and intent, she spoke from the heart about the power of collaboration. "We have to reevaluate the paradigm that the only way to solve our countries' problems is through violence," Mariam replied when asked about how to best end war in Syria. "But I cannot create a democratic Syria by myself, and I, myself, cannot change the world," she added, looking at each of the other panelists. "But by working together, we all have a chance."

At the close of the panel discussion, I introduced myself to Mariam and asked if I could interview her when she was back in New York City. She agreed, looking both humble and surprised.

A few weeks later, Mariam and I met at a small café near her office at the United Nations where she has served as representative of the Syrian National Coalition since 2013. The day of our meeting, she arrived modestly dressed in a brown top and black pants, her shoulder-length dark brown hair complementing her dark eyes. Her ivory skin did not house a hint of makeup. I asked her to tell me more about her work, particularly as a member of the Syrian Women's Political Movement (SWPM), which she helped launch in 2017.

"For too long, women in Syria have been boxed and cornered in civil society, education, and humanitarianism," she told me. "Whether it's been about elections, the constitution, or anti-terrorism, women have represented only about five percent of these groups. We will no longer be sidelined."

With over one hundred current members, 15 percent of them men, SWPM is run and led by women like Mariam, who influence UN policy. "Ultimately, we want to create a separate body, a women's political party, that will guide men rather than have them view us as competition," she said assuredly.

I was so impressed by the dedication and courage Mariam expressed the day of our meeting that I decided to include her as one of Women's eNews's 21 Leaders for the 21st Century in 2017. She humbly accepted, and during the night of the gala the following May, she again stood out. Honored among a revered group of twenty other women and men, including political leaders, foreign ambassadors, and leading artists and activists, she shared a number of tragic stories, one of which moved me above and beyond any other story I heard that night.

As she stood at the microphone, she spoke softly of a Syrian boy whose image she had seen in a photo. His lifeless body lay spread out on the street as bombs exploded all around him. He was covered in white dust. Not a soul was around to carry his body away from the carnage surrounding him.

"And he is one of just many, many we don't even know about," Mariam shared. This powerful story brought tears to Mariam's eyes, to my eyes, and to the eyes of numerous others in attendance. "Now the solution in Syria is to create a comprehensive peace, and no more killing on the ground!" Mariam exclaimed, her voice rising in strength. The entire audience rose to their feet in applause.

More than two years later, I met with Mariam again in the summer of 2019. This time it was to interview her for this book. We greeted each other like longtime friends. Again she dressed in dark, modest clothing. But she had a determination about her that seemed even more resolute than before. It had now been two years since SWPM was launched, and her organization's commitment to nonmilitary strategies to help rebuild her country was even more solidified. Six months after the SWPM held its first general assembly meeting in Frankfurt, Germany, the movement reiterated its commitment to continue to press on with the goal of creating gender equality in Syria by being part of a political process that guarantees the rights of all its citizens, women and men.

She told me exactly how they planned to do it, by establishing a comprehensive feminist plan involving five strategies: 1. Prioritizing public services, infrastructure, and utilities; 2. Identifying the needs of women, men, and youth; 3. Activating women's political and social participation; 4. Promoting, monitoring and accountability; 5. Reforming and amending property laws.

"We are collectively working toward creating a free and inclusive democracy and sustainable peace," she told me.

Once she had finished explaining the plan, she fixed her eyes on me. "We need to have an established party of very qualified, politically experienced women who are ready to jump on any new composition to take over in Syria," she said. "And we will not put a gun in any woman's hands."

Mariam then spoke about the United States' role in Syria, and how it used to take a leadership role in creating peace there. "But when Barak Obama became president, he said he did not want to intervene any more in Syria." She cast her eyes downward for the first time. "And now that Trump is president, it's worse. He just doesn't care about Syria or any of our policies. He seems to only care about taking down ISIS. At least with Obama, the US gave more humanitarian support."

In the vacuum that's resulted from this lack of commitment to Syria, Russia has taken the lead, which, according to Mariam, has resulted in the "killing of people left and right, with impunity." At this point she gazed back up at me, more intent than ever, and said, "The Russians don't care about human rights, they only care about keeping al-Assad as president."

Because of that, three and a half million people in Northern Syria's province of Idlib live under constant bombardment with nowhere to go. "All of the borders around Syria are closed," Mariam said. "Nobody wants refugees."

The need for a new constitution in Syria, where women are equal, is paramount. "This will enable women to be the executors, not just the policymakers, to ensure that decisions about health, education, and other basic needs are followed through," Mariam said. "These policies have to be gender-sensitive for every girl receiving medical care, for every girl receiving an education, for every single girl!"

Our time was up after an hour because Mariam had another appointment scheduled. Still, she didn't leave until she thanked me for being, as she said, a "catalyst" for the recognition of her work.

"You gave me that first award of recognition," she said, referring to Women's eNews's 21 Leaders award in 2016, "which made me feel a little more confident." Since then, she has been honored by numerous other organizations, including Apolitical (a global learning platform for government) as one of its 100 Most Influential People in Global Policy for 2019.

"You were the first person I thought of when I won that award," she told me as she gave me a long hug. "You made me feel, for the first time, that it's okay to be recognized publicly," she continued. "I now know that if I accept recognition, I will not shrink."

As we walked out of the café and said our final good-byes, I watched her as she raced across York Avenue among the yellow taxi cabs stopped in traffic, then quickly up the stairs to the entrance of the United Nations.

As I thought about our meeting, and about Mariam's unrelenting and all-embracing work to create peace in a country ravaged by war, one of my favorite Rumi quotes came to mind: "Out beyond ideas of wrongdoing and right-doing there is a field. I'll meet you there."

photo © Laura Fuchs

CAROL JENKINS

*"We need to make sure all women
have a clear shot at success."*

—CAROL JENKINS, copresident and CEO of
The ERA Coalition

Just opposite a prewar residential building in the Hamilton Heights section of New York City stands a huge iron plaque dedicated to Ralph Ellison (1914–1994). It reads: *American Writer, Longtime Resident of 730 Riverside Drive. His pioneering novel,* Invisible Man *(1952), details the struggles of a young African American man in a hostile society.*

Inside this building lives Carol Jenkins, another celebrated African American writer, and one of the first African Americans to serve as a television news anchor, a career for which she has won many honors, including an Emmy Award and a Lifetime Achievement and International Reporting Award from the National Association of Black Journalists, New York Chapter.

Today, she serves as the copresident and CEO of The ERA Coalition, a nonprofit organization dedicated to ratification of the Equal Rights Amendment. "I hope I live long enough to see it," Carol tells me.

I interviewed Carol just two days after she received promising news about the status of the ERA. Democrats in Virginia had taken control of the state's legislative bodies, and they planned to endorse the ERA. This would make Virginia the thirty-eighth and final state needed to ratify the ERA, a measure that was first approved by Congress and sent to the states in 1972.

"I want to see the ERA passed," Carol says, her eyes focusing intently on me. "It is a fundamental vehicle that we need to equalize women in this country."

Born in Alabama seventy-five years ago, Carol says of her childhood home that it was "the poorest county in the country, and it is still the poorest in the country." She continues, "My grandparents were farmers, and I credit my grandfather for being the feminist in the family. As the father of nine daughters, he would often say, 'These girls need equal footing in the world.'" All nine of those girls went to college, and that family ethos has since filtered down to four generations. "We all have him to thank for that," she says.

I was introduced to Carol over twenty years ago when she interviewed me on WNYW's Fox Five Live. At the time I was the publisher of *Divorce* magazine, a regional publication originally launched in Toronto, though it had a US presence. I had been hired to head its newly launched New York edition, and appeared as a guest on Carol's news show to discuss how divorced noncustodial parents could still stay in touch with their children on a daily basis by using the latest technology: fax machines.

Carol's career spans thirty years as a broadcast journalist, which has included national political coverage, reporting from the floor of a number of Democratic and Republican conventions. She also covered the release of Nelson Mandela from prison in South Africa, and coproduced a television special on apartheid, which was nominated for an Emmy award. Sitting in her home, which also serves as her office, the history of her work and accomplishments are present everywhere I look.

On the floor in front of me is a framed image of the iconic NBC logo, a peacock sprouting its feathers in multicolor, with the words PROUD AS A PEACOCK printed just below it. Standing on a glass shelf in one of her living room display cabinets is her Telly, an award for excellence in video and television. Hanging on the opposite wall alongside her desk is a banner that reads: MEET THE WRITERS: CAROL JENKINS AND ELIZABETH GARDNER HINES DISCUSSION AND SIGNING: BLACK TITAN: A.G. GASTON AND THE MAKING OF A BLACK AMERICAN MILLIONAIRE. Carol's coauthor is her daughter, Elizabeth Hines, and their book is a biography about Carol's uncle, A.G. Gaston, the grandson of slaves born in 1892, who died a highly successful businessman with a fortune valued at over $130 million. He created a path for numerous other African American businessmen to follow, and Carol has both honored and embodied his legacy.

Just below that banner hangs a photo of Carol with novelist Toni Morrison, who won the Nobel Prize for Literature in 1993. "That's one of my favorite photos," Carol says. A 1950s Oliver manual typewriter sits on a small wooden table in front of the window, and a sign with the word RETIRADO (Spanish for retired) stands upright on Carol's desk. But she is doing nothing of the sort.

Carol is, in fact, preparing for a conference call to discuss the successful passage of the ERA in Virginia with a group of women who've worked with her to get it passed. A printed page with the headline, "Ten Ways The ERA Coalition Makes a Difference," rests on her desk alongside her computer.

Now that the ERA has won its thirty-eighth state, Carol is concerned about whether they'll be able to remove the deadline for approval, since it expired many years ago. "We are working with Congresswoman Jackie Speier and Congressman Jerry Nadler to get the deadline extended. And Majority Leader Nancy Pelosi already promised to give us a hearing on this issue," Carol says, sounding confident. "It's still so complicated," Carol continues, betraying a bit of concern. "We are assuming this will go all the way to the Supreme Court, so we're working hard to get all fifty states to unanimously approve the ERA by working every week with the unratified states to get their endorsements."

Carol had informed me during our interview that she was planning for a conference call, and asked if I would stay and continue the interview after the call was over. I saw this as an opportunity to watch history in the making, and Carol put the call on speaker phone so I can listen in.

"Are you recovered?" one of the call participants asks all the others.

"I don't know if I'll ever recover," someone on the call responds. The women continue to congratulate each other one by one about Virginia's passage of the ERA. Carol is taking notes.

As I look around her living room, I am surrounded by row upon row of books adorning walls, tables, and desks. Some of them stand out to me more than others, many of them representing Carol's work and legacy as an activist for civil rights and gender rights. I see titles like *This Is an Uprising: How Non-violent Revolt Is Shaping the Twenty-First Century; Together We Rise: Behind the Scenes at the Protest Heard Around the World*, which chronicles the Women's March of January, 2017; *The Civil Rights Movement: An Eyewitness History,* which covers key years in the movement, from 1954 to 1965. And I notice one of my favorites, Mary Pipher's *Writing to Change the World*, which supports the idea that writing enables people to be transformed.

As the call continues with logistics about next steps, I stand up from the couch and walk around the apartment to look at the photos that grace her home. There are photos of her daughter and grandchildren, six-year-old twins, Sophie and Sam, and ten-year-old Avery. She moved into this apartment one year earlier to be closer to them. They now live in the same building.

I see a framed banner from the first "Take Our Daughters to Work Day" event on April 28, 1993. It reads: "If all you're told is to be a good girl, how do you grow up to be a great woman?" Next to these words are photos of such famous feminists as Gloria Steinem, Marie Wilson, Anita Roddick, Jessye Norman, and a nine-year-old Marlo Thomas alongside her celebrated father Danny Thomas.

As soon as the conference call ends, Carol looks up at me. "We scheduled these calls every week leading up to the vote in Virginia. We're hoping that the momentum in Virginia will reach to other states, where we'll be beefing up our efforts. Voters in other states need to learn what their state representatives can do for them."

I tell Carol I wish I'd brought a bottle of champagne to celebrate the Virginia vote. She offers to open a bottle of wine instead. As she pours me a glass, she says, "People in Virginia understood what was at stake, the future of girls and women across the US. The fact that we got it passed is just tremendous." And on that note, we toast.

I notice a record album lying on a table next to an old phonograph. It's Aretha Franklin's "A Brand New Me," recorded with The Royal Philharmonic Orchestra.

"That's a favorite of mine," I tell Carol. She takes it out of its sleeve and places it on the phonograph.

As Aretha sings in the background, Carol tells me that what women want most is peace in the world. She refers to the Women Media Center's SheSource, an online database of women experts for journalists to connect with, of which I am a member. "We have women in this database who could build an atom bomb if they wanted to, but they wouldn't do it. They want peace, not war," she says. "If we have a woman president, we will have a safer world. And now that there are women, Latino, black, and gay candidates, I feel this is the first truly Democratic race for president."

Carol then talks about the book she and her daughter wrote about Carol's uncle, A.G. Gaston. "He owned the hotel where Martin Luther King, Jr. stayed, and he once bailed King out of jail." His hotel is chronicled as an important part of the Birmingham Civil Rights monument and is now being restored. "The farm I was born on was also one of the stops in Selma during the civil rights march," she continues, "and the Black Panther movement started in that neighborhood." She tells me that she takes her grandchildren to Alabama every year for family reunions. "I even have a picture of Avery sitting on my grandmother's bed," she says, smiling proudly.

Carol looks around her living room, taking in some of the photos of her grandchildren that I'd been looking at toward the tail end of her call. "My next project is to put together a complete history of my family, from way back," she says, "and then end world hunger." She smiles at me. "As soon as the ERA is finally ratified."

LENORA LAPIDUS

"Dissent is patriotic."

—LENORA LAPIDUS, former director,
Women's Rights Project, ACLU

Lenora Lapidus was a lawyer with the American Civil Liberties Union (ACLU). For the past eighteen years she's led its Women's Rights Project, an initiative that was cofounded by US Supreme Court Justice Ruth Bader Ginsburg in 1972 to equalize women's rights under the US Constitution.

On May 5, 2019, at four-thirty in the morning, Lenora died from her fourteen-year battle with metastatic breast cancer. She was fifty-five years old. In addition to mourning her loss, I was distressed that I hadn't had a chance to interview her for my book. But then I thought, who better than her daughter to provide insight, stories, and experiences about her mother? I contacted Lenora's seventeen-year-old daughter, Isabel, who goes by Izzy. Since Lenora was a long-time Facebook friend of mine, it was not difficult to find Izzy online. I sent her a message requesting an interview, and we met one afternoon after school let out. Izzy is a senior at Fiorello H. LaGuardia High School of Music & Art and Performing Arts, the famous high school featured in the 1980 popular film, *Fame*.

Izzy is already seated at Lincoln Center's Prelude Café, just two blocks away from her school, when I arrive. She closes her laptop when she sees me walk in and tucks it into her schoolbag. She's a pretty young woman with bright blue eyes and long, wavy, blondish-brown hair. The powder-blue sweater she is wearing augments her eyes. Her mother had dark brown hair and eyes, but as soon as Izzy smiles, it's as if her mother were here in the room with us. It is the same smile: bright, warm, and welcoming.

I'd met Izzy three years earlier when Lenora and her husband, Matthew Bialer, brought her to Women's eNews's 21 Leaders for the 21st Century awards gala in New York City where Lenora served as one of our 2016 honorees. It was the first gala I'd hosted, and Lenora was honored for her activism for women's rights. As an attorney, she had worked at the ACLU for close to two decades, where she challenged and fought for the protection of women, even taking on major corporations in the highest court in the land, the US Supreme Court.

One such case involved an issue close to Lenora's heart— and her health. She worked with the ACLU to join forces with the Association for Molecular Pathology (AMP) to challenge Myriad Genetics, a major biotech company that was monopolizing the testing of mutations in genes that could increase risk for ovarian and breast cancer. Although the ACLU originally expressed concern that joining this case could impede future scientific research on other issues that impact women's health, Lenora took a stand. She believed the ACLU had an obligation to halt efforts to impede treatment for these two diseases. Furthermore, she argued, Myriad Genetics' monopoly was stifling research and increasing the cost of the test. The ACLU was ultimately convinced, and proceeded to file a lawsuit against Myriad Genetics in 2009. Four years later, the US Supreme Court also agreed with this assessment, marked by a unanimous decision in 2013. A photo of Lenora at the Supreme Court remains on her Facebook page. Her comment reads: "Here I am at the Supreme Court! Almost time for our argument in *AMP v Myriad Genetics,* challenging patents on the BRCA genes, which are associated with breast and ovarian cancer. Fingers crossed the Court will find the patents invalid!"

Other major cases Lenora took on, and won, included those defending female victims of domestic violence. In one case, brought on behalf of Tiffani Alvera, a woman who was evicted from her home in Seaside, Oregon, Lenora argued in court that applying "zero-tolerance against violence" policies to victims of domestic abuse is discriminatory because more domestic violence victims are women. Alvera had notified her landlord of the restraining order she had obtained against her husband after being assaulted by him in her apartment, and the landlord's response was to deliver an eviction notice two days later citing a "zero-tolerance policy" against violence. A settlement was soon reached, requiring the landlord to pay Alvera compensatory damages and agreeing to not evict or discriminate against tenants for being victims of violence.

In another case arguing for victims of violence, *Lenahan v. United States*, Lenora won a decision from the Inter-American Court of Human Rights, declaring that the US violated international human rights law for failing to respond adequately to gender-based violence.

As I sit opposite Izzy, I am amazed by the perpetual twinkle in her eye and the constant smile on her face. Yes, this is a teenager who lost her mom just six months ago, but it's clear that her mother had given Izzy so much confidence and hope.

"At home she was my biggest cheerleader," Izzy says about her mom. "I knew that when she wasn't at home, she was changing the world, but when she was with me, it wasn't about her at all. She was very subtle and modest about her work. I believe I came into my own at an early age because I was always supported to be who I wanted to be, rather than what she wanted me to be." Citing an example, Izzy recalls a story about her mom taking her to the monkey bars every day after school. "Although she wanted me to get all the way across those monkey bars, she would just stand back and watch. She knew I had to do it on my own. She helped me learn all that I am capable of, and now I don't stop at anything until I complete it."

Izzy then tells me that her mom's battle with breast cancer had been a constant throughout Izzy's life, and that she always had an understanding that her mom wasn't going to be there forever. The day before her mom passed, when it was clear that she was near the end, Izzy was walking in a park with two close friends. "I remember saying something about my mother not having to be there to know how successful I will be in the future. She already saw that the person I will be is the person I already am."

At her mother's memorial service, Izzy read a tribute to her mom. It appears as part of a collage of photos of Lenora with Izzy on Izzy's Facebook page. It reads:

"One of the many gifts my mother gave me was strength. She taught me how to look pain in the face and breathe through it; to feel and accept it rather than run away from it. She taught me that life would not be filled with people handing me whatever I wished for, and in order to get what I wanted, I had to fight. From a young age, she instilled the idea into me that I can achieve anything I want if I just try hard enough."

One of the photos in the collage also shows Lenora and Izzy at the Women's March in January 2017 in Washington, DC., holding up signs that read: DISSENT IS PATRIOTIC and WE THE PEOPLE, both featuring the ACLU logo.

I reminisced with Izzy about some of my own memories of her mother's kindness and thoughtfulness. When a mass email was sent out to Women's eNews's subscription list announcing my role as its new Executive Director in July 2016, Lenora was one of the first to respond. When I first invited her to be a guest on our radio show, Women's eNews Live, in June 2018, she couldn't appear because she was already scheduled to testify before the New York Department of Labor in support of One Fair Wage, which would eliminate the sub-minimum wage for tipped workers. "I'm sorry I can't appear," she wrote to me in an email. "I hope you are well."

Not long after, when she finally had a Wednesday morning available to appear on my radio show, she eagerly welcomed it. "I want to talk about the various factors that contribute to the gender wage gap, and legislative initiatives—at the state and federal level—that are being introduced," she wrote to me in advance of the interview. "These factors include lower wages, lack of transparency, salary history, occupational segregation, pregnancy discrimination, and lack of paid family leave," she continued. "I can also discuss our current litigation, particularly challenging pregnancy discrimination—and employers' lack of accommodations for pregnant or breastfeeding women, using anti-discrimination laws that already exist. How does that sound?" I told her it sounded great.

In the 2017 film, *Equal Means Equal*, a documentary exploring the need for the Equal Rights Amendment to be added to the US Constitution, Lenora and I were both among a number of women interviewed about the challenges women face in the quest for true equality. "The workforce is designed around the normative view of the worker as being a man who is married and has a wife at home who can take care of the family without that man needing to have any family responsibilities, and that notion really needs to change," Lenora says in the film. "It is important that, if we are really striving for equality, we need to open up the workforce to enable women to have an equal role, and to make family care and family responsibility more attainable for men and fathers who want to play that role."

Unlike her mom, Izzy, who is in the midst of applying to college, is not currently interested in becoming an attorney. "I am fascinated by astronomy," she tells me, her eyes widening. "I recently did an internship at The Museum of Natural History." Yet, just like her mom, she plans to transform this passion into helping other girls. "I want to use my interest in astronomy to further STEM education for girls. In fact, I am currently working on my first astronomy startup called Reach Up," she tells me. "I want to inspire children about space and am already planning to host a workshop at my former elementary school in Park Slope, Brooklyn, on STEM Day at the end of January next year. My interest in helping girls in STEM is because of my mom."

Lenora's lasting impression on women and girls has gone far beyond her immediate family, as evidenced in the accolades and tributes published and posted everywhere, from social media to the mainstream media. In *The New York Times*, a tribute appeared a few days after her passing featuring a photo of Lenora seated at her desk at the ACLU. On the outside of the front door hangs a large yellow poster with the words: BREAKING DOWN BARRIERS. FIGHTING FOR JUSTICE. Inside her office, on a bookshelf, stands another sign: LOVE TRUMPS HATE, just below a framed photo of her husband and daughter hugging. Below *The New York Times* photo is a quote from a colleague, referring to Lenora: "From custodians to nail salon workers to women in combat roles, she understood that the women's movement needed to be broader than the focus on white-collar professional women."

The ACLU has officially honored Lenora by naming its law library after her. On the outside wall, a square brass plaque hangs below a black-and-white head shot of Lenora, smiling brightly. It reads: "A courageous leader for women's rights, advocate for social justice, champion of human rights, and dedicated colleague, friend, and mentor. We salute her strength, wisdom, and optimism, against all odds." Ruth Bader Ginsburg sent the following personal message to her family: "I was so pleased and proud of the great work Lenora did at the helm of the Women's Rights Project. Her wise head and steady hand guided the project just as I hoped it would. Her bravery these past years was inspirational. May all to whom she was dear carry on in life in good health, just as she would have willed."

After I got home from my interview with Izzy, I logged onto Lenora's Facebook page and read a post that says: "Remembering Lenora Lapidus. We hope people who love Lenora will find comfort in visiting her profile to remember and celebrate her life." There's a recent photo of Izzy, her boyfriend, and her father. The caption reads: "This is the birthday weekend of Lenora Lapidus. Months ago, she purchased tickets for *To Kill a Mockingbird*, which she was eager to see. And so we went. And she would have loved it. Izzy's boyfriend, Nico, went with us in her place."

Yes, I nodded in agreement, she would have loved it.

photo © Foundation for Gender Specific Medicine

DR. MARIANNE LEGATO

"Women have a gift to give men that they can't refuse."

—DR. MARIANNE LEGATO, founder and director of
the Foundation for Gender-Specific Medicine

"Remember," Dr. Marianne Legato said when I interviewed her on May 17, 2019, "not only do we begin to ask—and answer—different questions about women's health by specifically studying women, but we also ask different questions about men's health as a result. For example, men, too, get breast cancer and suffer from osteoporosis—which most physicians didn't consider in the past."

I first met Marianne J. Legato, MD, PhD, FACP, an internationally renowned pioneer in the field of gender-specific medicine, two weeks earlier at an intimate gathering over brunch at the New York City home of Loreen Arbus who is, in her own right, a fearless pioneer and champion for the rights of the marginalized, particularly for women and people with disabilities. Also in attendance were a number of other powerful and philanthropic women, including Alice Walton, the daughter of the founder of Walmart and board member of the Walton Family Foundation; Penny Abeywardena, New York City's commissioner for international affairs; Whitney W. Donhauser, president of the Museum of the City of New York; and Elizabeth Kabler, daughter of the late Leonore Annenberg, the former US chief of protocol for President Ronald Reagan.

I'd read all of these women's impressive bios, and still it was Dr. Legato's that caught my attention, due to her success and prominence as the founder of the Foundation for Gender-Specific Medicine, an organization she established to study gender differences to improve healthcare for everyone. A number of news outlets were then reporting on Caster Semenya, the South African transgender athlete who lost her case against the International Association of Athletics Federations when they ruled that she must take medication to lower her testosterone levels if she wanted to continue to compete in global running events. Since Women's eNews was planning to publish an article on this topic, I was looking forward to asking Dr. Legato about her thoughts on this controversial issue. "I am actually writing a book about this right now," she replied. I was not at all surprised, and immediately asked to schedule an interview with her.

On the cutting edge of all things related to gender differences in medicine, Dr. Legato's previous best-selling books have included *Why Men Never Remember and Women Never Forget*, *Eve's Rib: The Groundbreaking Guide to Women's Health*, and *Why Men Die First*. It is through Dr. Legato's pioneering research and discoveries, in fact, that doctors have come to understand the differences between how women and men experience the same diseases, including heart disease and stroke.

Yet, how Dr. Legato first came to dedicate her career to gender medicine was accidental, I later learned. The day of our interview,

I was welcomed into her Upper East Side Manhattan practice by her office staff, and I noticed the mutual respect between them right away. As she introduced me, she commented on their extraordinary dedication to her center's work. Proceeding into her private office immediately afterward, she did not sit behind her large wooden desk surrounded by stacks of medical books, but alongside me in one of two same-size chairs, with framed photos of her family and friends in the background. She wore a bright orange dress adorned by a simple gold necklace, and her shoulder-length, light-brown hair rested gently on her shoulders. Her eyes, beaming behind frameless oval glasses, were focused yet warm. After I thanked her for taking the time out of her busy schedule to meet with me, she replied, in a voice that was both gentle and purposeful, "I always say yes to every reasonable invitation."

It turns out that this is exactly how Dr. Legato first came to focus on gender-specific medicine. "I was a molecular biologist doing research on the human heart for the American Heart Association when a journalist asked if I would conduct research about potential differences in women's heart disease, which had caused her mother's death," Dr. Legato recalled. "I really thought there was no difference at the time. Wow, was I wrong!" The results of her research resulted in her prize-winning book, *The Female Heart: The Truth About Women and Coronary Artery Disease,* published in 1992. This caused her to wonder whether other female organs in the body were also different from those of men. She smiles when she recalls her revelation: "Maybe women and men really are different!"

This could not have been more surprising to her, since she had been trained in the medical tradition that proclaimed: "If we only studied men, there was no need to study women separately, because we assumed that, apart from their reproductive biology, they were functionally identical," she said. The first studies on human physiology were originally compiled on men only because they were thought to be more stable (without the cyclic hormonal changes of women), were readily available in veterans' hospitals following both world wars, and were always ready to volunteer for medical studies. "No one ever thought to suggest that we were making an intellectual mistake by only studying men," Legato continued. "In a real sense, we exploited men, who were always willing to join clinical trials in spite of the possibility that they were at a certain amount of risk in doing so. Even though we concentrated on men, our questions often didn't address their most fundamental vulnerabilities: Why did men die at significantly younger ages than women, for example?" It was originally thought that women suffered coronary artery disease when they were ten years older than the age at which men did due to the protection of estrogen. However, when men were given estrogen, it proved fatal in the doses chosen, and studies on preventing coronary artery disease in men were abandoned." Legato said. "But there had been no previous research about the differences in the cardiac function of men and women that would have predicted this would happen."

As much as Dr. Legato's career in medicine led to tremendous gains in the medical community for women and men, it also resulted in some personal losses for her, due to her family's deep-seated patriarchal beliefs. The only daughter of four children, she told me, "My father wanted his second son to become a physician, just like him. So, when I became the physician, instead of my brother, it created a permanent rift between us." She persisted in spite of her father's lack of support; he remained intransigent and refused to attend her medical school graduation. Her father told her brothers that she was no longer his daughter. "Yet, I do think he loved me; he was enchanted by me as a child," she recalled. "It was only when it came time for me to oppose him and become a physician that he withdrew his support for me." Her father required his entire family, including her mother, to join him in opposing her medical training, which they did, except for her youngest brother, Gerard.

Even though she grew up under such a misogynistic family structure, she did not allow these experiences of disappointment, rivalry, and loss to cause her to lead a life of anger and resentment. "I've come to understand that people do what they want—not what they should do, nor what we hope they will do," she said. "If they're fearful of being abandoned, or of a child surpassing what they have achieved, they may find those relationships difficult, and there's nothing we can do about it." And it was through understanding who her parents were—what frightened them, and what threatened them—that she ultimately forgave them. She said of her youngest brother, Gerard, "He has been invaluable in helping me understand the intricacies of my family's relationships with one another, and helped me to accept that my parents were truly unaware of how hurtful they were to me." She dedicated the prize-winning third edition of her textbook, *The Principles of Gender-Specific Medicine,* to her brother.

But Gerard was just one of the caring and compassionate individuals who lent their support to her life and career. While studying at Manhattanville College, the school's dean often reiterated the motto: "Do the truth in charity." Legato said, "That simple sentence taught me the twin values of justice and compassionate generosity in dealing with others." Legato put this teaching into practice after her award-winning book, *The Female Heart: The Truth About Women and Coronary Artery Disease,* was published in 1992. "After winning the competition sponsored by the American Heart Association for the best book published for the lay public on heart disease, one of the judges called and asked me to become a consultant for Proctor & Gamble. He thought my input would be valuable as a consultant for products that would improve women's health." Instead, she told him she had a better idea. "Tell Proctor and Gamble that an alliance with Columbia University College of Physicians and Surgeons would be a much better idea than my individual contribution; it would give P&G access to all of the science in the world on this topic." she recalled. They did just that and, as as a result, P&G ultimately funded Legato's ongoing research to the tune of four million dollars. "This is an example of giving back in the best way that you can. I could have had a great job as a consultant for P&G, but this alliance was much better and broader." The support of P&G allowed Legato to establish the Foundation for Gender-Specific Medicine, now in its twenty-third year.

Even now, as an internationally renowned academic physician, author, and lecturer, Legato does not, by any means, believe that she is "fully formed." She told me, "I always have gaps to fill . . . to be more generous, to be more realistic, and to be more effective." This is what she tells her students in her role as professor of clinical medicine at Columbia University College of Physicians and Surgeons. "I urge them to say *yes* to every opportunity, just as I do, and to try to be open-minded and open-hearted in their responses to challenges."

"The trouble in life is that you can't live it all over again once you've learned everything you need to know," she told me at the end of our interview. "Too bad we can't redo everything." Yet what she has done in her career, by refusing to allow her patriarchal upbringing to limit her ambitions, or to lessen her compassion and generosity for others, has enabled her to develop an entirely new arena of medical research that has changed the lives—and saved the lives—of countless women and men.

photo © Nadia Todres

SUZANNE LERNER

"Giving is the best investment I've ever made."

—Suzanne Lerner, social impact philanthropist,
entrepreneur, cofounder and president of Michael Stars,
the Los Angeles-based fashion company

I first met Suzanne at the Women's eNews's 21 Leaders for the 21st Century Awards Gala in 2012. I then began seeing her speak at a variety of other women's empowerment events in New York City, often discussing what employers can do to support gender equality. In 2017, the first year I hosted the Women's eNews's annual gala as its executive director, Suzanne was selected as one of our twenty-one honorees. In 2018, she served as one of our gala's cochairs.

She invited me into her New York City pied-a-terre in Chelsea to interview her for this book in October 2019. She met me at the door wearing all black, a silver pendant in the shape of a circle with the words DREAM BIG hanging from a silver chain around her neck. Her dog, Ms. Simba, a wheaten terrier who goes by the hashtag #feministpup, nestled next to me on the couch as we started the interview.

It's easy to be in Suzanne's presence. She's candid and warm at the same time. I'd use the word "effortless" to describe her, much like the casual, iconic styles her fashion company, Michael Stars, is known for. Her generosity shines through her bright blue eyes and long, reddish-brown, wavy hair.

We caught up briefly about an inspiring event we both just attended at the annual Women's Media Center Awards Gala, a nonprofit organization launched by Gloria Steinem, Jane Fonda, and Robin Morgan to call out sexism in the media.

As we settled in, Suzanne told me how exciting it was to witness new generations of women connect to Michael Stars' purpose and vision, as well to its contemporary fashions. "We've always wanted to help women feel empowered to use their voice and speak out. It's amazing to see new generations of women connect to that vision and support us."

Suzanne cofounded Michael Stars with her business and life partner, Michael Cohen, who passed away in 2015. When they met, Michael was working with local artists to print vintage poster art on T-shirts. He asked her to represent his line, and when she saw its potential, she worked with him to more fully develop it. They began with the simple purpose to make fashion that was timeless, effortless, and comfortable. What started with the iconic one-size-fits-all and one-size-fits-most premium T-shirt has evolved into a collection of well-crafted, beautiful contemporary essentials.

Suzanne and Michael also envisioned the potential for their company to create opportunities for their local community. Michael Stars was an early innovator, locally sourcing and manufacturing its clothing in Los Angeles, which gave them direct control over garment quality and the ability to ensure fair wages. The company also became a platform from which she could support gender equality.

"The first year, we knew that our company was going to be about more than fashion. And, when I look back on it now," she said, "I realize that it was finally my chance to build something where I could bring together all the values I cared about."

I've known Suzanne for nearly ten years. But I didn't know how she rose to become who she is today. I asked about her childhood years, which she described as growing up in a hard-working Jewish family of "modest means and big dreams." "Most of the women in my family worked. There were very few stay-at-home moms," she recalled. "They did all the work of a homemaker, but they also had full-time jobs. Mom was an accountant, and I don't think she ever considered not working. "

The youngest and only daughter of three siblings, Suzanne's parents, and particularly her mother, gave her crystal-clear advice growing up: "Get an education. Go be what you want to be. But you still have to learn to type so that you'll always be able to support yourself, no matter what!" Suzanne's rebellion against gender-based limitations started as a child. She recognized early on that as a girl she would have to fight for things that were granted automatically to her brothers.

"It was assumed that my brothers would go to Hebrew School," she recalled. "My parents told me that I could go too, but I'd have to choose between that and the Girl Scouts because they couldn't afford both. I chose Hebrew School to be just like my brothers." She laughed, unaware at the time that her choice would require four nights a week of study after school for four years. "It cut into my social life in a big way," she continued, "But I lobbied so hard to attend that I could hardly quit." She stuck with it and four years later was one of just a handful of girls at that time to have a bat mitzvah, the Jewish coming of age ritual.

Her penchant for activism and philanthropy began at a young age, influenced by her family's values and the dynamic social movements for gender and racial equality in Chicago. "Social change was all around me and I knew I wanted to be part of it," she said. "Even though my parents wanted us to work hard, they also felt it was important to give back. I started out by collecting change for UNICEF. Then, when I was old enough, I became a tutor on Chicago's South Side and a volunteer at Cook County Hospital. There was a shortage of support in those communities. It started to open my eyes to the racial inequality that was being reinforced by segregation. I knew I didn't want to live in a world like that."

In high school, she signed on for a student exchange program that would allow her to spend a semester at one of Chicago's inner-city high schools, made up of primarily African American students. Those students would then spend time at her suburban, primarily white high school. "I never experienced a minute of trouble during my time there. Yet when those students of color came to my school, it was very different. There was bullying and intimidation, fueled behind the scenes by threatened parents," she recalled. "They were sending a message: This is our school and you're not welcome here. It was full-force exposure to racism and racial inequality."

Gender bias would also come into play for Suzanne as she started working as a secretary during her high school summer vacations. "Of course, I could type pretty well by the time I was sixteen, so I worked in various offices around Chicago. The first thing I noticed was that every office was led by a white male boss, and there were mostly white women in support roles," she continued. "They were expected to serve every one of their boss's needs. There were also very, very few women of color in professional positions in any of the offices I worked in."

By the time she became an undergraduate student at the University of Wisconsin, Madison, Suzanne said that "both my eyes were already wide open" to racial injustice around the world. Much to her parents' dismay, she dropped out after her freshman year and went on the road, traveling to Nepal, India, Australia, Europe, and many other locales.

Ironically, her mother's insistence that she learn secretarial skills proved invaluable. "I literally typed my way around the world," she said with a laugh. "No matter where I traveled, I could always find a job. I was able to support myself in every country I lived in. It enabled me to continue traveling, which was the real education I'd been craving."

She grew into what she calls a "full-fledged feminist" during her years of international travel. "Everywhere I went, I saw women of all cultures struggling for an equal place in society. I realized then that gender equality was truly a global issue," she said, although her rising consciousness didn't make life easy—personally or professionally.

While in Australia, she lived with a "good looking" Australian surfer. "He had blond shoulder-length hair and was a lot of fun. He wasn't put off by my being a feminist," she recalled. "But when we would go to the pub to meet his friends, he'd leave me to sit with them, while I was expected to drink in the ladies' lounge. I guess I wasn't much of a lady because I wasn't about to sit in a segregated lounge. I decided to rally all his friends' girlfriends to join me in breaking the rules. His 'bro' pals didn't like that very much!"

Professionally, Suzanne soon took the bold step of starting her own business. Her first venture was a fashion import business from India which brought her to Los Angeles. A friend connected her to a mentor whom she described as "fashionable and formidable." She mentored Suzanne and helped teach her the business from the ground up. That experience propelled Suzanne into the fashion business, and ultimately inspired her to become a lifelong mentor herself.

When her first business didn't succeed, she rejoined the fashion business as an employee but quickly became frustrated as the doors of advancement were continually slammed in her face. She found that she was consistently passed over for promotions that were given to men with less experience, while she was relegated to roles like "showroom girl." Even though her first fashion business had failed, she struck out again on her own, convinced that there would greater long-term opportunity if she ran her own business. She was right.

By the time, Suzanne cofounded Michael Stars with Michael Cohen, she had become a successful serial entrepreneur with several businesses already under her belt. The eventual success of Michael Stars enabled Suzanne and Michael to establish the Michael Stars Foundation, which has since become a major supporter of organizations that build critical pathways to equality in the US and abroad.

Yet even while running her own business, Suzanne experienced another major battle with gender bias when she took over as president of Michael Stars after her husband passed away. To most this would seem like a natural transition, leading the business she had cofounded, yet there were skeptics inside the company who suggested that the firm might need more "experienced" leadership.

I ask her what it felt like, especially in the wake of dealing with the loss of her husband, Michael. "It was really difficult," she admitted. "Michael had been the face of the company, while I was knee-deep in merchandising, sales, creative, and design, among other things. There were people inside the company who had no idea how experienced I actually was in the fashion business. I'm not even sure whether, if they had known, it would've mattered. I wasn't given the benefit of the doubt that a man in my position would have been given."

Suzanne still took the reins and did what she felt was needed to drive the company forward, which included making it "classically female." "I tore down silos that had formed over the years," she recalled. "I rallied people to work together and rewarded collaboration. Even the skeptics became supporters.

Today, I have a great team, great products, and a purpose, vision, and mission that we work toward every single day."

As Michael Stars and its foundation continued to grow, Suzanne began to develop a gender lens built around supporting grassroots organizations, informed by her experiences as an entrepreneur, business leader, and activist. I could see the excitement in her eyes as she described two transformational experiences that inspired her approach. The first was during her trip to Haiti in 2011 with the Women Donors Network to witness the devastation and the massive recovery work resulting from the earthquake there. Not one to just observe, she quickly became involved in the relief effort.

"In the midst of all that devastation, I saw the incredible resilience of the Haitian people. In every community I visited, there were core groups of women working together with many healthcare providers, artists, actors, and businesspeople who showed up to help. That experience showed me the importance of partnering with communities."

Her second experience occurred during a luncheon with a number of feminist women, including Gloria Steinem. Suzanne soon realized that the gathering was not just a lunch, but a fundraiser for the Ms. Foundation. As Gloria spoke during the event, Suzanne found herself growing more and more inspired, so when Gloria finally got to "the ask," as they say in fundraising, an extraordinary thing happened: "Gloria said they had thirty-nine women, each of whom had pledged a million dollars to the foundation. She was one short of her goal of forty. I jumped up and claimed number forty. It was like an out of body experience," she said with a huge smile.

She also marked it as the beginning of a friendship with Gloria. "When I introduced myself to her after claiming the fortieth spot, she was thrilled. I thought it was mostly because of my donation, but it turns out she had been a Michael Stars fan for years! That day felt so good!" It was an important milestone for

Suzanne, having realized that all the hard work building her business had brought her to that important moment—stepping forward to make a significant commitment to supporting gender equality.

Those experiences also marked the start of a more fully developed gender lens investment strategy that Suzanne created to make decisions about every aspect of her investments, from personal finances to philanthropy. "Gender lens investing has redefined my entire perspective. I've elevated my approach beyond traditional methods to invest in companies that are diversifying their leadership to include more women," she continued. "As an investor and entrepreneur, I love seeing data that shows companies with more women in leadership roles improving their financial performance. As a human being, I love that I can play a direct role in improving the lives of women and girls by investing in their businesses."

Suzanne's current philanthropic focus is to support grassroots organizations where women of color are building local, national, and global platforms to advocate change in the constructs of power to enable gender equality. Her background as an entrepreneur and activist draws her to these smaller, more nimble organizations. She sees them as efficient and resourceful, but seriously under-resourced.

"Women—especially women of color—are leading grassroots organizations that are incredible forces for empowerment and social change," she said. "Typically you'll find that they have developed broad and deep networks and a high level of trust within communities. They also understand the cultural, social, and economic barriers to creating change, and in many cases have been working for years on ways to overcome those obstacles. Yet only a fraction of foundation and individual giving is targeted to women of color who lead grassroots nonprofits. That has to change."

We then came to a pause in the conversation. She glanced at her watch to tell me what else was on her plate that day. Meetings

at her showroom to review plans for a new Michael Stars collection, calls with several social impact entrepreneurs seeking
her advice, and meetings with her team to plan several women's
empowerment events over the next several months were all on her
agenda. And, of course, Ms. Simba was in need of a walk outside.

As she led me to the door, she handed me a beautiful, pale
pink scarf that she selected for me. "One more really important
thing," she told me as we stood at the door. "It's our responsibility to share what we've learned with new generations of women
and help them become business and social justice leaders, as well
as philanthropists. There is a misperception among some women
that philanthropy is about having a lot of money to give away,
and that it's something you do only when you're older. Don't get
me wrong, writing a check, whatever the amount, is important.
But giving of yourself matters just as much."

She hugged me good-bye and added, "Giving is the best
investment I've ever made."

Bella Abzug (left) with Dianne Dillon-Ridgley (right), photo © Dasal Ridgley

DIANNE DILLON-RIDGLEY

"Women are most impacted by the issues surrounding climate change, and we're the ones most apt to stop it."

—DIANNE DILLON-RIDGLEY, environmental activist and former executive director of the Women's Network for a Sustainable Future

When Dianne Dillon-Ridgley speaks, people listen. Perhaps it's because of her bold and commanding voice; perhaps it's because of her strong presence (she's often draped in bright colors under a head of wispy silver hair); or perhaps it's because she's able to seamlessly infuse into conversations inspirational quotes from books and speeches that have long inspired her, little dashes of daring and defiance. I suspect it is all three.

I interviewed her by telephone on a Saturday morning in January 2020, and even though she was hundreds of miles away in her home state of Iowa, her presence was as commanding as ever. Dianne is a lifelong advocate for sustainability and first entered the environmental field as a college intern for the Environmental Protection Agency in the early 1970s. "I have a ferocious commitment to the truth, particularly about the damage we are doing to our planet," she told me at the beginning of our phone call. "Just as Rachel Carson wrote in her 1962 book, *Silent Spring,* which exposed the long-term damaging effects of pesticides like DDT: 'Can anyone believe it is possible to lay down such a barrage of poisons on the surface of the earth without making it unfit for all life?'" Dianne continued, "We are at a tipping point."

For Dianne, women's rights and fighting for environmental sustainability are intertwined, now referring to parts of India and Africa as examples. "Women have been the water carriers for eons. Young girls have to sacrifice going to school so they can carry the water home for their families. Women's eyesight has been damaged from cooking and cleaning over hot steaming cookers with no ventilation," Dianne told me, her voice steady. "This is just one of many environmental exposures that hurt women, and we are only beginning to learn the extent of the damage." That's also why she believes that women will be the ones to save our planet. "Women are more apt to stop people from doing things that put short-term economic gains ahead of our long-term needs," she added.

I first learned of Dianne when one of the magazines my company published, *Green Matters,* was seeking nominations for its annual Green LEED-ers Awards in 2010. *Green Matters* was a bimonthly publication that featured news, trends, and analysis about the importance of sustainable design in real estate construction and development. Dianne's name came up time and time again due to her passionate commitment to sustainability in building and construction, so I decided to honor her. At the time she was a member of the board of directors of Interface, Inc., a global manufacturer of modular carpet, where she served from 1997–2014. "When Ray Anderson, founder and CEO of

Interface, Inc., asked me to join the modular carpet manufacturer's board of directors," she said during her acceptance speech as a *Green Matters* honoree later that year, "he phrased the question like this: 'Will you come help me change the world?' 'Well,' I replied, 'I've already been doing that for years,' so it seemed only natural to join him." Dianne continued speaking to the two hundred people in attendance, who seemed captivated: "I really believe as humans, we are hardwired to be in nature, so our buildings need to be beautiful and functional in ways that make us feel that we are in nature, whether we're in the heart of Iowa or in the heart of Manhattan."

During her speech she also quoted Bella Abzug, the feminist and environmental rights activist who served as a US congresswoman for New York from 1971–78, and founder of the Women's Environment and Development Organization (WEDO), where Dianne later replaced her as CEO: "In my heart I've always believed women will change the nature of power rather than power changing the nature of women!"

In early 2019, when Women's eNews was planning to honor women leaders in sustainable design, Dianne sent me a copy of *Women in Green: Voices of Sustainable Design,* by Kira Gould and Lance Hosey. The book opens with a question, "Is There a Green Gender?" and then answers the question affirmatively by positing the authors' findings: "Our conversations with architects, designers, and educators find that women are more likely than men to support environmental causes through voting, activism, and consumer choices."

Dianne had written the foreword, which she'd titled, "In Time," and which begins like this: "Why women and sustainability? Look throughout history and mythology. It relates to being a mother with a sick child—vomiting, diarrhea, the works—it's not glamorous. The mess won't go away and clean itself. You take a deep breath and get busy caring for your child. It's not that fathers cannot or do not. Many do. But the world over, for centuries, caring is what mothers and all women have done. And this is true of women leading change now. The mess is there. We are the mothers and midwives of this twenty-first-century effort to care for our world. As we said in 1991, when more than fifteen hundred women and 'non-women' from eighty-three countries gathered in Miami at the World Women's Congress for a Healthy Planet: 'It's time to mother earth.'"

"Yes!" Dianne said when I referred to this paragraph on our call, "When I wrote it's time to mother earth, I used 'mother' as a verb. She has been here for thousands of years, and we have abused the earth. We have to stop that!"

As further testament to the unyielding strength and power of women, Dianne spoke about the heroine in the book, *American Jezebel: The Uncommon Life of Anne Hutchinson, the Woman who Defied the Puritans*, a biography written by Eve LaPlante in 2010. It documents the life of Anne Hutchinson, who, in the seventeenth century, was charged with heresy for pushing social reform and gender equality. As she stood in front of forty male judges, pregnant with her sixteenth child, she defended herself at a time when women did not have the right to vote or hold public office. "She ended up being exiled from her home state of Massachusetts, and the judges were still so threatened by her unorthodoxy that they built Harvard College to maintain the religious and male social order of that day," Diane told me. "This was revelatory to me, how she stood up to those judges back then. It still inspires me."

Dianne told me a bit about her own ancestry. "I was an only child and only grandchild with two incredible grandmothers who set me on the path of understanding how 'women do it anyway.' Regardless of our challenges and battles," she explained. "I was taught that women find a way to correct problems. Often women will turn it on its head—they'll take a situation, whether intuitive or automatic, and work to solve the problems." She said she learned this early in life when one of her grandmothers sent her books by George Sands (born Aurore Dupin), a famous yet controversial woman writer in nineteenth-century France who rebelled against society's gender norms, who refused to compromise her personal life (she was bisexual and often cross-dressed) or her writing, which included raw themes of sex and sexuality.

Another of Dianne's grandmothers was a college professor who graduated from Tuskegee University in 1919. "Imagine a woman, let alone a black woman, getting a college degree in 1919," she said with pride. "I have a picture of her from her college yearbook. George Washington Carver was her faculty advisor."

She then told me that earlier that week she'd been thinking about a "combination of things about how to put a stop to climate change." She said, "I was considering what policies we need to have in place and what do we need to change in the private sector, along with how we rear our children and subsequent generations to make saving our planet a priority." She then answered her own questions. "It all comes down to the same answer: We need to get people to stop doing things that put our short-term economic gains over our long-term needs."

Dianne believes that parents, as children's first teachers, are key, and relayed a story to me, told to her by a friend of hers years ago: "There was a girl who played in the streets of Kenya with the tadpoles. They each had colorful little beads on their heads, and she wanted to take them out, but her mother told her, 'You shouldn't do that since you would be preventing the tadpole from becoming the amphibian it is.' Instead of scolding her daughter, the mother educated her to understand the bigger picture and the result of her actions. She taught her how to admire something without destroying it," Dianne said, explaining the moral of the story. "This is how women do it."

She then brought up Greta Thunberg, the Swedish environmental activist who recently said during an impassioned speech at the United Nations Climate Summit in 2019: "I shouldn't be up here. How dare you! We are in the beginning of a mass extinction, and all you can talk about is money and fairy tales of eternal economic growth. How dare you! The eyes of all future generations are upon you. And if you choose to fail us, I say, 'We will never forgive you.'"

"And she was right," Dianne continued. "She shouldn't be the one to tell the world what to do."

Still, Dianne is concerned that far too many are stepping back into the comfort of business as usual. "There is so much evidence to show us what is happening to our planet. We don't need more information to convince us. We need more collective courage."

As our interview came to a close, Dianne told me that she had to get ready for a meeting later that day with Katie Porter, the Democratic US congresswoman who had held to account some of the most powerful people in the country by taking on the big banks. In one of her tweets soon after her election, she wrote: "Climate change is an existential threat to humanity, but Donald Trump and @RepMimiWalters are deep in denial." Republican Mimi Walters lost to Katie Porter in the 2016 election and has since been named chief commercial officer of Leading Edge Power Solutions, LLC, a distributed energy resource company.

"One of the things I say whenever I speak publicly is, 'We spent the last forty years trying to politicize the environment, but that was the wrong mission. We should have been environmentalizing politics!'" She had one more thing to add: "The unique power of women is that we don't tend to do only one thing at a time, which has always been the problem with most men—doing only one thing at a time. It is the interconnectedness that is going to be our salvation."

photo © Leandro Justen

S. MONA SINHA

"It is not about us versus others. It is about what we can all accomplish together, regardless of the color of our skin, or where we were born."

—Mona Sinha, feminist, activist, philanthropist

I had met Mona Sinha a number of times over the past few years, always at one of the various women's empowerment events held at posh ballrooms in and around New York City. We often only had enough time for a brief "hello" before another attendee would grab her attention to discuss their latest project. It was not until I was invited to a Sunday brunch at the home of Loreen Arbus, a long-time champion for women's rights, in early May 2019, that I finally got the chance to hear, first-hand, her personal narrative about what led her to devote her work, and her life, to supporting women and girls around the world. Since her story was unlike any other I had ever heard before, I immediately asked her if I could interview her for my book. She welcomed me into her home just a few weeks later.

"When Mother Teresa told me that she didn't need me anymore, I cried," Mona Sinha recalled, as she began talking about her childhood. She had been volunteering part-time at Mother Teresa's orphanage in Calcutta, India, since she was a sixth grader. After graduating from high school, she planned to spend significant time as a volunteer during the months that she had before the start of college. Initially saddened by her response, Mona soon realized that this was the best advice she could have been given. "Just as she encouraged the children in her orphanage to explore the world, she did the same with me," Mona said, showing me a signed photo from Mother Teresa along with her handwritten message, *"God Bless You."* It led instead to her work with disabled children at the Spastics Society of Eastern India, sparking a love for supporting the underprivileged. Down the road, it shaped her life as a gender rights advocate and mentor to hundreds.

Calcutta is a long way from New York City's Upper East Side, over eight thousand miles to be exact. Yet as I sat in Mona's home, her motherland was present in everything from its décor to Mona's outfit. She was dressed in warm orange and brown earth tones, her dark black hair pulled back, her dark eyes deep and soulful. She leaned against one end of a long beige couch, and I sat at the other, taking note of the small statue of a stallion standing atop an antique brown wood table just behind her. The stallion, I thought, served as the perfect metaphor for the majestic way Mona presented herself—a woman of modest stature yet clearly in command; oozing kindness, but with a firm grip on how she navigates injustice and creates systems for change. Old family photos appeared in vintage frames throughout her home. Before we had sat down together, she showed me some of them, picking up one of her great-grandmother in particular. "She was nicknamed Tigress," she told me. "I come from a long line of strong women."

Then there was her grandmother, a woman who, she said, "knew how to shoot a rifle, smoke a cigar, play bridge, and mix drinks, all at only fifteen years old." Married to the son of the city's chief of police (under British rule), her grandmother had to quickly learn how to become a gracious hostess to her father-in-law's British colleagues and friends. Her husband, a lawyer, however, was a nationalist fighting for freedom. They lived in the same home, which presented a conundrum. "Her life changed during the independence movement of the late 1940s, where she was the gracious hostess during the day, but, at night," Mona told me, "she would sneak out of the house and drive into town with her husband, despite the curfews and amid the mounting riots, and they would secretively bring wounded activists back to their basement to be tended to. After all, who would think of looking for them in the police chief's home?" It's no wonder that people in her city soon began referring to her grandmother as Florence Nightingale. Very strong, both brave and bold and able to live this double life.

Although Mona wasn't aware of her foremothers' extraordinary levels of compassion and courage until later in her life, she was fortunate to witness these qualities in another woman who would become her early inspiration, Mother Teresa. In the overpopulated and impoverished city of Calcutta, Mother Teresa started a new order in 1950, The Sisters of Charity, to help those who she felt were the "forgotten human beings," providing homes for orphans, lepers, the dying, and the destitute. It brought safety and dignity to their lives.

"When I was a schoolgirl in sixth grade, I was chosen to bring the crafts we made to the children at Mother Teresa's orphanage," Mona recalled. "When I first stepped through its doors, I was blown away. I never knew there were kids my own age living there." Though Mona described the scene as "chaotic," filled with lots of noise, babies crying, and kids running around freely, she added, "All you felt was love, deep love everywhere." She said that while these kids had very little in terms of material possessions, they were still happy. Yet it was here that she first saw gender discrimination. "Given male preference in our society, many of the boys were adopted, while the girls got left behind," she said.

Calcutta was a special place to grow up, where she saw everyone, regardless of caste or creed, living together as a community. Mona attended midnight Mass on Christmas Eve every year without associating it with Christianity and celebrated Eid with her Muslim friends in great anticipation of the delicious meals that were shared together. Across the city, everybody came together to celebrate the Goddess Durga for five days each year as the powerful symbol of feminine strength. Even today, Muslims care for the synagogue, as few Jewish people are left in the city. Despite that, women and girls were often discriminated against, and male preference was prevalent in her own family of three daughters. "Calcutta is where the seeds of who I am developed." It was by nurturing her innate compassion and generosity that Mona was also emboldened to shift the reality of discrimination.

Mona's true courage was tested when Indian Prime Minister Indira Gandhi was assassinated in 1984, prompting her to leave her country. "I was already attending an excellent university there," she said, "but classes were disrupted due to the political chaos, so I knew I would have to get an education somewhere else." Determined to go to an all-women's college in the US to fully explore her burgeoning feminist core, she ultimately attended Smith College in Massachusetts on a full scholarship. "Smith College had its first female president at the time, Jill Ker Conway," Mona said. "I had read her book, and she inspired me. Gloria Steinem was also a graduate. I knew this was the right college for me."

But there were more ways to be inspired and much more to learn beyond the walls of Smith College. She recalled feeling "free but also frightened out of my wits," by having to learn how to fit into a new culture with no family support. There was a new lesson to learn every minute, and this was particularly the case when she met her advisor, who was also the chair of the Economics Department, Professor Cynthia Taft-Morris. "I went to a reception at the president's house, and this very tall woman with crutches—she'd had polio—walked right up to me, lifted up one of her crutches, and said she was looking for me," Mona recalled. Taft-Morris was eager to meet Mona after learning of her background in Calcutta, and of her courage to travel all the way to Smith alone for an education. She then took her house key off her key ring, gave it to Mona, and invited her to have tea with her the next day. As another Smith professor said, "If Professor Taft-Morris loved you, she had your back; if she didn't, you knew it right away." That meeting turned into years of Taft-Morris's guiding, supporting, and mentoring her, although Mona was not aware of the professor's lineage at first, as the grandniece of former US President William Howard Taft. "I kept that house key with me every day until I graduated," Mona recalled with a smile. Smith unlocked many treasured experiences including meeting and working with Gloria Steinem, whom she described as her "North Star." In return, Gloria recently described Mona in the following way: "Mona lives in a world without boundaries . . . as a citizen of the world, she has always seen people as linked, not ranked." Ultimately, Mona served as a Smith College trustee and helped shape and guide the largest-ever capital campaign for a women's college, raising close to half a billion dollars.

While a student at Smith, Mona was encouraged to discover her true promise, and she afforded the same to others in return. Even after building a successful early career in one of the most competitive, male-dominated industries, investment banking, Mona's philanthropic roots never faltered. "I chose a career in banking because I wanted to feel financially secure and learn some real financial skills," Mona told me. While working at

Morgan Stanley, her first job out of college, she quickly built a solid reputation. After business school at Columbia University, she moved to Unilever, where she learned about brand building and innovation by working on such iconic brands as Vaseline Intensive Care and Pond's. Ultimately, she moved to Elizabeth Arden (a Unilever owned company at that time) to rebuild the Asia Pacific Oceania market. "I was in my thirties, and I would spend more than half the year in Asia." She says that during this time, she had to utilize both business and life skills, be at once demanding and encouraging, while reshaping the businesses in diverse markets. Her teams across the world had to trust her in tough financial times as they worked on turning around their businesses. Many years later, several of them stay in touch, a testament to her leadership.

"Fundamentally, I am successful because of my restructuring background in business. I can see where the holes are. I can read a business plan and see what pivots are needed," she said. "Once you assess the biggest gaps, you see where the opportunities lie." During her time with Unilever, she was spending six weeks in Asia and then four weeks at home. "It was exhausting and exhilarating at the same time, but definitely not sustainable. I had no time for family and had to make some tough decisions."

Therefore, when she was provided with an opportunity to accelerate her career even further, she decided against it. "I knew, deep down, I didn't want this as a long-term career," she told me. "It was time for me to use the skills I'd learned as a negotiator in banking and restructuring businesses to build sustainable organizations with leaders who could change the world, as I had been taught to do from the beginning in Calcutta."

And that's exactly what she has been doing for the past twenty years. Leaving investment banking to enter the non-profit world, she has mentored hundreds of women, particularly around the impact of education and economic independence. She has also invested financially in many entrepreneurs. "By attending Smith College, I learned the importance of education, and what it can do for young women," Mona said, now sitting more upright. "I can see what these women are capable of achieving even before they do. I want to be like Professor Taft-Morris in their lives." This mission has led her to become a founding member of the Asian Women's Leadership project, which is focused on empowering women as future leaders in Asia. One of her mentees wrote in a card she shared with me, "I am so thankful for you as a mentor and friend. Thank you for believing in me when I did not believe in myself. Your incredibly inspiring spirit is so needed in this world."

She also recognizes where there is a need for leadership and steps in. When the Science and Nature Program, which serves underprivileged girls (and others) at the American Museum of Natural History, was in danger of closing down, she raised the funds to help it grow, and today it educates hundreds of children in science. Her love for Calcutta is manifest through her board work with Apne Aap, an anti-trafficking organization based in India, where she brought her daughters to visit a safe house for prostitutes and participated in a group art project with the kids. A few years ago, she and her children traveled with Gloria Steinem to the lower Zambezi, where she is still involved with projects that enable women to be economically independent. "I gained a daughter, Alice, who is a leader in her community," she says with a smile. "She makes me so proud by working to stop child marriage and give young women a chance at living a full life."

Mona is also the board chair of Women Moving Millions, an organization dedicated to mobilizing unprecedented resources for the empowerment of women and girls by each member committing a million dollars to advance gender equality. In 2017, she cofounded Raising Change, Inc., to teach mission-driven organizations how to raise resources for social change. She serves on numerous other boards as well, including the Tamer Center for Social Enterprise at Columbia Business School, the

Columbia Global Mental Health program (a collaboration with the World Health Organization), and Breakthrough, a human rights and justice organization. More recently, her activism has taken root as a board member of the ERA Coalition, which is pushing Congress to ratify the Equal Rights Amendment to the US Constitution for the first time in history.

While doing so, however, she has not lost sight of the impressionable impact she is making as a woman of color and a representative of immigrant people. "When I represent these organizations and speak publicly on their behalf, I am showing that it is not about us versus others. It is about what we can all accomplish together, regardless of the color of our skin or where we were born," she reflected. Her leadership has been recognized with many awards including the 2015 Ellis Island Medal of Honor.

In 2020, Mona is planning to place a greater priority on funding grassroots women leaders who are making systemic changes with little outside support. "They can make real change because they are proximate to their work," Mona said. "That is the lesson I learned from Mother Teresa and the leaders I now work with. These changemakers need our strong support because they are pushed down by patriarchal systems everywhere." She then showed me an article she printed out for me, "Philanthropy for the Women's Movement, Not Just 'Empowerment,'" published in Stanford University's Social Innovation Review newsletter on November 4, 2019. It reported that women's and girls' groups received only 1.6 percent of US-based charitable giving in 2016, and that US foundation funding for foreign groups that advocate for gender equality dropped from 30 percent to 15 percent from 2002–2013. "We cannot allow this to happen," Mona warns. "If you want the world to improve, you must believe in women as the true agents of change."

In addition to helping others, she also holds a deep commitment to her own family. As a wife and the mother of three children, she proudly told me, "My husband and son are feminists, as are my twin girls." She has been married for over thirty years to her childhood sweetheart. Just then, her son stepped into the living room where we were sitting, wearing a T-shirt with the name "Brearley School," an all-girls school, emblazoned in bold letters across its front. "He wears one from Smith College as well," she said, smiling at him.

She then turned to one of her two golden retrievers, Charlie Brown, a certified therapy dog who had been lying on the sprawling antique rug draped across the hardwood floor throughout our interview. "You see, even he serves others, just like every one of us should. Both my dogs are my personal therapists, helping me think clearly as we go on our early morning walks."

LINDA STEIN

*"What does it take to turn a bystander
into an upstander for justice?"*

—LINDA STEIN, artist, activist, educator, performer, writer

When walking into Linda Stein's art studio in Manhattan's Tribeca neighborhood, you never know how you will experience her art, or how her art will experience you. Some will find themselves putting on full-length wearable sculptures, made with everything from metal zippers to seashells to copper coins. Linda's artwork allows visitors to explore strength, gender, and empowerment by wearing her work, often wrapping themselves in a kind of body armor similar to that worn by fierce female superheroes like Wonder Woman.

"Wonder Woman protected the weak and downtrodden in a nonviolent way," Linda told me, explaining why she chose Wonder Woman as one of the female icons to include in her

"Fluidity of Gender" exhibition, which explores the continuum between power/vulnerability, femininity/masculinity and warrior/peacemaker while inspiring compassion, empathy, and bravery. "Wonder Woman is an excellent example of anti-bullying and gender justice," Linda told me. Just like Wonder Woman, Linda believes every woman can be an everyday hero. "I invite the viewer to 'try on' personal avatars, which encourages them to engage with their more audacious and authentic self."

I've visited Linda's art studio many times in the decade that I've known her, and every time I enter, I see something new. Through her nonprofit organization, Have Art: Will Travel!, Linda's traveling exhibitions, in addition to "Fluidity of Gender," have included "Holocaust Heroes: Fierce Females," which features female heroes from the time of the Holocaust in large sculptural tapestries, and "Displacement From Home: What To Leave, What To Take—Cabinets, Cupboards, Cases, and Closets," which represents Linda's take on issues of global displacement, sanctuary, and safety.

When I walked into her studio in the fall of 2018, I was struck by the power of a new tapestry hanging in the middle of a long horizontal white wall. Within Linda's series called "Sexism: Exploring, Exploding, Expanding Expressions of Masculinities and Femininities," one tapestry, "Legs Together and Apart," displays images of women sitting with their legs apart, a defiant exhibit exploration that challenges society's beliefs about how women sit, how women take up space, and our cultural double standards for women and men. "This is objectification and catering to the male gaze," read one comment written on the tapestry.

"In interviews and videos, women have revealed to me long-harbored hurts and guilt related to this issue," Linda said. She then told me a story from her childhood. "I was about nine years old, sitting in a neighborhood park with a bunch of boys and girls talking, laughing, and having fun. All of a sudden, in front of everyone, one of the boys jumped up from a bench and touched my genitals. I was shocked. I turned bright red and I asked him why he did that. He told me that I was sitting wrong. My legs were open and that gave him the right to do it, he said."

Linda's story reminded me of an experience I had as well. As I started to speak, she stopped me and asked if I'd be willing to stand in front of the "Legs Together and Apart" tapestry and allow her to record me on her iPhone. I told of an incident I had long repressed of being sexually assaulted by my brother.

"When I lived at home, my family and I would always move into the living room after dinner. We had a long, light-brown couch facing the television set, and one night my mother lay down at one end and my brother sat upright at the other, leaving a small space for me to sit between them. As I lowered my body to sit, I felt my brother's hand underneath me, grabbing my crotch. I jumped up immediately, shouting at him to move his hand away. He laughed but kept his hand there. My mother, who witnessed it, said nothing. And then it happened again, a few days later, but this time my father was there to see it. 'You don't do that,' my father told him, in an unusually gentle and questioning tone. This time my brother did take his hand away, chuckling and seeming a bit embarrassed. Again, my mother said nothing. Sometimes I still feel the shame and disgust from his violation, and the entire family treating it like it wasn't a big deal."

Telling my story to Linda in her studio while standing in front of that tapestry made me feel free, relieved, even empowered. "Art can open minds. It can put people in touch with thoughts long repressed, and start conversations from its visual/visceral stimuli," she would later write in an article published in Women's eNews. In it she linked to the video she'd recorded of me telling my story. I felt proud and grateful to finally expose my truth and release the shame of that long-buried incident.

Earlier that year, Linda had been honored as one of Women's eNews's 21 Leaders for the 21st Century. The awards gala was held at the Museum of the City of New York, a historical art museum located on Fifth Avenue directly across from Central Park on what is known as Museum Mile, which houses seven museums along its mile-long stretch. Linda was dressed in one of her custom-designed heroic vests, another example of her wearable art. The front of the vest shows Wonder Woman pointing to her head and asking, "What defines bravery? What makes a hero?" The answer is revealed on the back side of the vest: "Bravery is not the lack of fear. It's proceeding in spite of it." Other words like BLAM! and CRASH! are emblazoned in bold bright colors throughout the black vest. Another question is posed: "CAN WONDER WOMAN CRA--AC-AK GENDER STEREOTYPES?" in multicolored green, red, and purple against a bright yellow background. She calls this series her "Bully-Proof Vests," and they all contain slogans against bullying and harassment of others based upon their sex, race, orientation, and abilities.

Linda is white, with short, red spiked hair and an athletic build. Her voice is gentle and assured. She delivered her speech, on the topic of accepting otherness, to a crowd of two hundred. Unlike each of the other honorees who stood at their respective tables to speak when receiving their award, Linda had asked if she could do hers in front of the entire audience. She walked to the front of the room, initially turned her back to the audience, and placed a black-painted Band-Aid horizontally across her forehead. She then turned to face the audience and proceeded to tell this story: "My friend came to my house wearing a beige Band-Aid across the forehead of her beautiful dark brown skin. I was taken aback, realizing for the first time that a variety of skin tones in cosmetics and Band-Aids were not readily available for people of color. I excused myself and came back to my friend wearing a black Band-Aid in the same place as hers, and suggested we go into town this way. I walked with my friend down a main street with this black Band-Aid on my forehead in contrast to the beige Band-Aid she was wearing," Linda said, pointing to it. She talked about the stares, the double-takes, and even the smiles of onlookers as she and her friend passed by, and onlookers realized that the two women were visually making a statement. "Imagine having to wear something designed for a skin color that is different from your own, with few other options," she continued. This experience was eye-opening to many in the audience. She had them all riveted as she continued with her interactive talk. "This is just one example of how something as simple and common as a Band-Aid can start conversations stemming from visual and visceral stimuli," Linda concluded as she ended her speech, accepted her award, and walked back to her chair.

Linda's art not only reflects issues of protection and otherness, it echoes the need for safety and sanctuary. In October 2019, I meet with Linda once again in her studio to interview her for this book. This time, I asked her to talk about her series of sculptures and collages called "Displacement from Home: What to Leave, What to Take—Cabinets, Cupboards, Cases, and Closets."

"This is of particular interest to me," I tell her, "since in October 2019, Women's eNews began publishing a monthly series of personal stories written by high school students who have crossed mountains and deserts and rivers to rejoin their parents in the US." I tell her that the series has caused me to think a lot about what I would do and what I would take with me if I had to flee my own country.

A look of sadness clouds Linda's face. She lifts her hand and places it gently on my arm. "When I created this series, I was hoping it would start conversations about asylum seekers, refugees, and our country's immigration policies. I also hope it will encourage people to speak up in defense of others."

She tells me about her experience on September 11, 2001, which caused her to be displaced from her Manhattan home for eight months. "Running from the falling Twin Towers that day, I found refuge with a friend at the other end of Manhattan. My apartment was covered with dust and debris, forcing me to throw out my couch, carpet, curtains, books, fixtures, furniture, and mattress," she recalls. "It caused me to think very deeply about the issue of being displaced due to violence," she says. "What would I take? What would I leave behind?" The series includes suitcases overflowing with small personal objects, like a spoon and a seashell, as well as cabinets with drawers filled with ribbons, a belt, even a bicycle wheel. "It's my hope that when someone looks at each of these cherished personal items, they feel compassion for the person who has to flee." She points to what appears to be the bottom of a broom with blue needles sticking out from a halfway-closed drawer. "Could you imagine what it must be like for people trying to cross borders, unable to return home, who must start again?"

She then looks back at me, her eyes expressing concern: "My experience, though traumatic for me, is inconsequential in comparison to those who were, and are, desperate to leave countries like Rwanda, Syria, Afghanistan, Iraq, Somalia, Ukraine, and regions like Southeast Asia and Latin America; as well as in our own country during the Great Migration when African Americans left the South, the Japanese in internment camps, and the Trail of Tears when the Cherokee Nation was forced to leave their homelands east of the Mississippi and resettle in Oklahoma," she continued. "I recall a woman who came to one of my museum exhibits showing "Displacement Cases." I was standing nearby as she looked mesmerized, staring at my pieces. I noticed tears coming to her eyes, and I walked over to ask if she was okay. She said this art made her remember the pain she felt when she had to leave so many cherished possessions behind as she fled her home for safety. There was a good chance, she said, that she might have to swim part of the way, and therefore could take nothing of importance with her."

It is through this series, as well as others, that Linda continually asks the hard questions, determined to ensure that we also ask ourselves: What does it take to turn someone from a bystander into an upstander for justice?

photo © Whitney Brown

MARCY SYMS

"Women must be equal under the law!"

—Marcy Syms, entrepreneur, author,
and president of the Sy Syms Foundation

first met Marcy Syms at the Democratic National Convention
in Philadelphia in 2016. I had just taken over the role of executive director at Women's eNews and had been invited to the
Feminist Majority Foundation's luncheon, where Marcy was
speaking. I was looking forward to meeting her, not only because
she'd been a long-time supporter of Women's eNews, but also
because I'd been told by many members of our staff that she was
one of the nicest people I'd ever meet. They were right.

As Marcy spoke on stage, she appeared warm and engaging,
her wide, bright smile never faltering. She greeted me with the
same wide smile when I introduced myself after her speech. It
was clear that she had that rare quality of being able to make

new acquaintances feel like old friends. She even smiled when she spoke about the frustrations she experienced in her crusade to get the Equal Rights Amendment added to the US Constitution, an issue that was and continues to be close to her heart.

I interviewed her for this book in December 2019, just one day after an event Women's eNews hosted on the subject of workplace equality. I recalled her seeming optimism, how she smiled even in the face of hardship, and she told me, "I love people, I always have." This seems to continually provide her with an upbeat nature which, in turn, naturally draws people to her.

The event Women's eNews hosted the day before included three panel discussions: equal pay, hiring and retaining female employees, and unconscious bias. Funding for the event had been made possible by the Sy Syms Foundation's Excellence in Journalism Program, an annual program created by Marcy Syms that provides funding to Women's eNews to train aspiring female journalists in the pursuit of journalistic excellence and investigative reporting for five straight years.

"For a democracy to flourish, all voices must be heard," Marcy said upon launching this program in 2014. As of the writing of this book, Women's eNews has gone on to train one dozen reporters in the researching, interviewing, writing, and editing of articles on the subject of gender equality and social justice through a local, national, and international lens.

Marcy and I met for the interview in my Upper West Side Manhattan apartment. When, early in our conversation, we spoke about the importance of women having their own money, I told her I first learned this important lesson as a high school sophomore when I read Virginia Woolf's *A Room of One's Own*.

"I love Virginia Woolf," she replied. "I wrote my college thesis on her."

I stood up in search of two old books I own—a 1932 edition of *A Room of One's Own* and a 1928 edition of Woolf's *Orlando*, two of my most prized literary possessions. As she leafed through them, I rummaged through a number of other shelves searching for my 1938 edition of *Harper's Bazaar,* which published a short story written by Virginia Woolf called "The Duchess and the Jeweler."

We looked through the magazine together, marveling at the advertisements, mostly fashion ads targeting wealthy women, which represented most of the magazine's subscribers at the time. There were many ads from Bonwit Teller, the Manhattan-based, women's high-end clothing store that famously stood at the corner of Fifth Avenue and 56th Street from 1930 to 1980. The entire magazine and its ads were in black and white. One ad displayed two elegant, thin white women wearing items from its spring collection, standing poised beneath the phrase: "We present the spring fashions destined for importance." Another showed three women, again all of them white and thin, in "Matinee and Teatime Fashions." Yet another showed four more women sporting "Chic by Seaside" style wearing "Stunning Beach Pajamas." We found humor in the ads, but were also dismayed as we realized so many products targeted to women and girls today still portray them as ideally white and thin, and needing to be told how to dress appropriately by others.

I then told Marcy that I remembered watching her family's department store ads on television. Her father owned a popular clothing store in New York City called Syms, though it served an aspirational clientele. Back in the 1980s, Marcy Syms would often appear in the Syms commercial. "An educated consumer is our best customer," was the tagline, and Marcy explained to viewers how the company marked down the cost of its unsold items at regularly scheduled intervals to make them more affordable to their customers. In 1983 when the company went public on the New York Stock Exchange, Marcy became the president of the corporation, the youngest person to ever run a publicly traded company.

Marcy, now in her sixties, is the oldest of five brothers and sisters. "Being the oldest turned me into my siblings' caregiver,"

Marcy told me, "but it also taught me how to delegate fairly, which gave me great organizational training I use all the time in managing people in business and philanthropy."

Marcy also learned something much more compelling, something that she viewed as illogical and unfair—that women were treated differently, unfairly, both at home and in the workplace.

She made it one of her early missions to change business practices at the company once she became the employer of hundreds and eventually thousands of workers. Speaking to the illogical part of her experience, she shared, "When the chores were divided up between my mother and my father, my mother did the household work, cleaning, ironing, and the like, and my father did the carpentry," she told me. "This made no sense because my mother had much more natural inclinations for carpentry than my father. As a girl, I was given all the inside chores as well, whereas my brothers were able to do the outside work like packing up the garbage, raking the leaves, and plowing the snow."

Marcy said she continually wondered why she wasn't allowed to do any outside work. "It was completely illogical, irritating, and wasteful because I could have been helpful to my brothers."

Despite these traditional gender roles instilled in her family's home, Marcy's father, Sy, learned early on to appreciate the advice of women. "He was the youngest of ten children, six of whom were girls, so he was preconditioned to listen to women's advice, which they gave him often," she said with a chuckle. She suspects this made him more receptive to her observations as well. "Although he was quite traditional in some ways, he didn't box himself into believing only one way, which included not prejudging women and men." He also taught Marcy to always question norms, and that if she sees something illogical to say something about it, and then change it in areas where she can influence change.

Marcy came to work with her father in 1978, almost twenty years after he opened his first clothing store. Marcy was in her late twenties and a college graduate with a master's degree who had worked in the media business for a few years. The store was expanding into women's apparel, and her father asked her to be the voice of a radio commercial he was planning to run. Not only did Marcy do that, but she created an entire media plan for the radio commercial. "That's when I knew I wanted to work for the company full time," she says. As she took on greater responsibilities, she also corrected things in the company's culture, including making sure that female and male employees did the same jobs. At first, her father was against it, even though he supported Marcy's abilities in other areas. "He was just convinced that men didn't want to be fitted for a suit by a woman," Marcy recalls. "I told him, 'Are you kidding? Most men would love to have a woman measure their crotch.'" Marcy went on to institute a "one-store concept," where there were no jobs that were exclusively female or male. "And there was no such thing as 'demeaning' work. Everyone had sweeping detail," Marcy continues. As a result, the company's work culture changed. Employees experienced new things, developed new skills, and found out what they were best suited for. "By continuing to rotate the jobs they would do, they also didn't get stale while doing any single one of them," she added.

By the early 1980s, the business had grown to eleven stores in four states, and after twenty-five years, to fifty-two stores in sixteen states. "On the day of our public offering, I stood right next to my dad to ring the opening bell at the New York Stock Exchange," Marcy recalls. "It was a very gratifying moment."

Once growing beyond its New York City roots, Syms was in a position to become a role model in its giving as an early supporter of community involvement, and by establishing a business school at Yeshiva University in New York. "Dad was particularly proud of this," Marcy says. Over three decades, the family's foundation has been hugely supportive of Public Television and Radio, PBS and NPR. It has also helped to originate programs like Frontline and Washington Week.

As an officer of the Sy Syms Foundation, Marcy also started to engage in her own philanthropic interests. "I always knew that gender inequality wasn't addressed in important areas of American society," she says. Just like when she was a child, Marcy felt this made no sense, so she made gender equality—and specifically getting the Equal Rights Amendment ratified—her greatest crusade.

"I had known Congresswoman Carolyn Maloney since her first run for Congress, and when she placed the Equal Rights Amendment imperative in front of me, I took up the fight full throttle," Marcy recalled. "She had set in motion the reintroduction of the Equal Rights Amendment, first proposed in Congress in 1923 by suffragette Alice Paul and introduced every year since then. Decades later, the ERA was finally passed by Congress in 1972 and then went to the states, where the legislatures would vote on ratification. But by 1982, the deadline established according to the Constitution, we were still three states short of the requisite two-thirds needed."

Marcy undertook a more formal role with the formation of the ERA Coalition and the Fund for Women's Equality, serving first as a board member and then as board chair. Today, through the efforts of Marcy and these two organizations, one more state needs to ratify the Equal Rights Amendment, and it looks like it will be Virginia in 2020. Congressional leaders in the House of Representatives have already marked up legislation to extend the 1982 deadline, and it is ready to be voted on.

"Gender justice is overdue," Marcy told me. "Not having an ERA is unfair. It's also insulting, and it enrages me, but I'm comfortable with the rage because it's appropriate, and the energy I derive from it is being put forth in a constructive way that will ultimately move things forward in the right direction," she adds, while still exuding a positive and assuring energy, just like she did the first time I met her. "We must have a society that includes equality of opportunity to fulfill our potential as a democracy."

CHERYL WILLS

*"What you love you will give your time to.
I'll take that to the grave!"*

—CHERYL WILLS, award-winning television
news reporter and anchor

I t is almost impossible to live in New York City without having heard the name, or seen the face, of Cheryl Wills. An award-winning television reporter and news anchor, she appears five nights a week as host of her own nightly news show, "Live at Ten," on Spectrum's NY1, one of the city's most-watched local news stations. Yet, it's her goal to ensure that her last name of Wills becomes known far beyond the streets of New York City, and for far more than just personal glory. In fact, she is on a mission, she told me, "to make a wrong right, no matter what."

Her ancestors, the Wills, worked on a plantation as slaves, where they were buried in unmarked graves. She's come a long way from the cotton plantation of Mooreland County, Tennessee, where her great-great-great-grandfather, Sandy Wills, served as a slave, and where the former slave shack still stands. Yet her ancestral history is present within her, permeating Cheryl's commanding presence and all-knowing smile.

"Digging into my ancestry has given me a sense of worth and pride like nothing else," she told me during our interview, as we sat together in the station's towering boardroom overlooking the massive newsroom below. Cheryl wore a sleeveless lavender summer dress, complementing her glowing mahogany-colored skin. She looked ready to step in front of the camera at a moment's notice, though it was only four in the afternoon, and her live show wouldn't begin until ten o'clock. She's used to appearing on air throughout the day to introduce scheduled topics and guests, and on the night I interviewed her, she'd be discussing coverage of Donald Trump's latest tweets where he called the City of Baltimore "a disgusting, rat- and rodent-infested mess," while sparring with the Reverend Al Sharpton after he responded that Trump "has a particular venom for blacks and people of color."

I interviewed her just a few days after a video of her went viral, in which her reaction to a fellow anchor's comment about Donald Trump crashing a wedding at his New Jersey golf club was widely shared. After her colleague remarked, "You have to say that was pretty cool that he stopped by . . ." Cheryl did not respond. Instead, keeping it cool and professional, she immediately moved on to the next news story. Her reaction was shared tens of thousands of times on Twitter, and replayed on numerous national news sites for days.

The day of our interview was not the first time I'd met Cheryl or observed her as a woman who stands up for what she believes in. This includes speaking out for the rights of others. Serving as a speaker, presenter, and honoree at numerous events dedicated to empowering the marginalized, she had been honored by Women's eNews as one of its 21 Leaders for the 21st

Century at our annual awards gala just one year earlier. She brought her mother as a guest, and upon receiving her award, she dedicated it to her ancestral family who, she said, provided her with "a warrior's DNA" to make her voice stronger and to help her realize the standards she must live up to.

Those ancestral standards were initially as much a surprise to her living family members as they were to her. When her father died in a motorcycle accident on Brooklyn's Williamsburg Bridge when Cheryl was just thirteen, she was surprised to see on his death certificate that his city of birth read Haywood County, Tennessee.

"I was born in New York City," she told me. "My father was born in New York City. So was my grandfather, my great-grandfather, and my great-great-grandfather. Nobody ever talked about Haywood." But once she learned about her heritage, she felt changed. "That birthed in me the desire to reconnect," Cheryl told me. "After that, I referred to the rest of my life as 'Cheryl Wills A.D.'"

In 2009, she first discovered that she was the great-great-great-granddaughter of an enslaved man named Sandy Wills who had fought in the Civil War. "I was shocked that no one ever talked about him and his bravery. My father and grandfather didn't even know about him, which saddens me," she continued. Yet, this was understandable, since after the Civil War ended, many black soldiers, who were still without sanctuary, were warned by their military sergeants to lie low and not talk about the war. "Sandy was a marked man for breaking away from the plantation and joining the Union Army. I know that he and his wife, Emma, must have lived in a state of terror at that time," Cheryl said.

Her mission then became to find out where Sandy and Emma were buried so that she could finally provide them with a respectful memorial. "They deserve to have headstones, and to be buried in a real cemetery," she asserted. Yet her broader goal is not only to memorialize her ancestors, but all slaves, particularly those who fought in the Civil War. "This ungrateful country allowed our soldiers to be buried anonymously because it did not see black people as full human beings, and when you don't have a firm identity, it's easy to throw your life away," she continued, now moving forward in her chair. "There is an epidemic in this country," she said. "We don't know who we are. Black children need to know that their ancestors were much more than just slaves. They were brave, they were smart, and they were heroic."

So she traveled back, way back, to the plantation where Sandy Wills served as a slave. "It was surreal to stand there and view the same landscape and horizon he saw when he was picking cotton in those fields," Cheryl recalled. The plantation's grounds still look exactly the way he left them, where cotton continues to be grown, picked, and sold. The plantation's owners, who are direct descendants of his slave owners, tried to scrub the plantation clean," Cheryl said.

"I believe they are fearful," Cheryl continued. "I believe Sandy and his wife, Emma, are buried there, and I will prove it. I plan to hire an archaeological crew to dig up each of those graves, and get every bone tested. And when I find Sandy's remains, I am going to give him the military funeral with honors that he deserves." Until then, Cheryl has paid tribute to Sandy on the written page, through the publication of three books she has written in his honor: *Die Free: A Heroic Family Tale* (2011), *The Emancipation of Grandpa Sandy Wills: A Children's Book* (2015), and *Emancipated: My Family's Fight for Freedom* (2017).

Paying tribute to her great-great-great-grandfather is only half of the story. The other half is equally important, if not more so. Emma Wills, who was married to Sandy, was courageous in her own right. "She was smart, and she was pissed," Cheryl told me. As the widow of a military man with nine children, Emma heard that the white widows were receiving their husbands' pensions on a monthly basis, but that the widows of black soldiers were not. So she filed an application, submitted all of the paperwork, and detailed her life as a wife and mother to the government. "Still, they refused to pay her," Cheryl said, "until one of the plantation owner's sons, Joel Moore, offered to help Emma provide proof of Sandy's birth and Emma's marriage to him."

Finally, in 1891, Emma was awarded her husband's pension. "Joel had to sign her name for her to make it official, since it was illegal for slaves to learn how to read or write," Cheryl recounted. "A space was left between her first and last name for Emma to place the letter "X." She scribbled that letter, which was her way of saying that she was no longer at the bottom of the barrel. This is a women's empowerment story if ever there was one." Cheryl smiled proudly at the image of Emma's actions.

Yet Cheryl considers the "X" she scribbled to be a metaphor for many others. "It is shared by countless other black girls and boys who have no idea where their ancestors came from," she said. Bent on a mission to change that, Cheryl has decided to speak; to speak directly to children and teenagers at schools throughout the United States, and particularly to girls who feel disempowered, whether they be in some of the highest performing schools on Long Island, New York, or in the lowest performing schools like Mott Haven in the Bronx. "Regardless of whether these children are homeless or living on a plush estate, I teach them the same story, and their responses are always positive," she continued. "What bowls these girls over every time is when I tell them about Emma's courage, so my fourth book is going to be written about her, and bear her name as its title," Cheryl said. "Although I haven't yet exhumed Emma's physical body, I have exhumed her bravery and her strength, and now I am using her as an example for current and future generations." Cheryl looked determined as she stated, "She mattered, and now everyone will know about her through my next book entitled *Emma*."

Cheryl believes that those in power have made use of a "trick of disempowerment" by getting black people to think that there were no brave and successful people in their families.

"That makes you think you have to start from the beginning, like you're building the wheel for the very first time, which can become all-consuming," she said.

To counteract this, Cheryl hopes to create a foundation, The Sandy and Emma Wills Foundation, to provide scholarships to people who, as she put it, "have lost their way." Its goal is twofold: To provide educational scholarships to people who show a desire to succeed, regardless of their academic grade point average, and to travel with students from low-income areas to the west coast of Africa, where there are untouched landmarks showing the history of slavery. These landmarks include the Island of Goree in Senegal, which served as the largest slave trading center on the African coast from the fifteenth to the nineteenth century, and Cape Coast Castle, built in 1652 to serve as a slavery trading post for many European nations. "I can tell them that this is exactly the way it looked when black families were trafficked from West Africa and brought to the United States," she said. "This will teach young black people that they came from somewhere, where their ancestors had a strong culture and traditions. Perhaps this will teach them to stop repeating the 'N-word,' one of many words white supremacists called their ancestors when they turned them into slaves."

Still, Cheryl's direction doesn't come without its critics. She has heard a lot of pushback in the form of, "Who do you think you are?" during her lifetime, not only for becoming a powerful black woman, but also for trying to get her ancestors memorialized with respect. She imagines this is similar to the pushback Emma got. She told me, "And I'm proud of her for sticking to her guns, and now I'm expanding upon the 'X' she used, as the only signature she could provide, by my being excellent, by my being extraordinary, and by my being exceptional." She looked at me contemplatively and added, "Never by being angry, but by being my very best, just like her."

JAMIA WILSON

"Helping other people realize their dream of publishing a book is also a dream come true for me."

—JAMIA WILSON, publisher, The Feminist Press, CUNY

There is often one book, at least one book, that forever changes a person's life. For me, it was *My Brilliant Career*. Published in 1901, it became an award-winning film eighty years later. It's a timeless book that I discovered at a seminal time in my life—as a student at the City University of New York's (CUNY) women's studies program in the late 1970s. It was required reading—and watching—for the Women in Anthropology course I was taking my junior year.

The "brilliant career" in this book is that of a young woman who defies family tradition to choose the life of a writer over being the wife of a wealthy man. The protagonist was a headstrong free spirit whose dreams were frowned upon by society, but that only caused her to increasingly long for, and further fight for the freedom she craved. It spoke to and inspired me at the age of nineteen as much as it does today, forty years later.

"A real book is not one that we read, but one that reads us," wrote the English-American poet W. H. Auden.

It's books like these that shape young lives, that point so many of us in a much-needed direction for our futures. And because of my time at CUNY, I was introduced early to CUNY's The Feminist Press, launched a half-century ago, just eleven years before I graduated.

CUNY has long been hailed for providing one of the finest public college educations in the country. Yet it's much less known for being the first college in the US to offer a major degree program in women's studies, a program from which I graduated in 1981. Its pioneering decision to add women's studies as a major was not at all surprising when you consider that CUNY was also the first to launch a feminist book publishing arm over a decade earlier, one that still exists today.

The Feminist Press has published feminist classics for years, from Charlotte Perkins Gilman's *The Yellow Wallpaper*, which it republished in 1973, to today's Amethyst Editions, a queer imprint launched in 2016 that champions emerging queer writers who employ gender-bending narratives.

I first met Jamia Wilson in 2015. We ran in the same circles through our connections at the Women's Media Center and Women, Action, and the Media (WAM). In 2016, she was hired as the publisher of The Feminist Press, the first woman of color to hold this position. She'd always been a strong presence whenever I'd encountered her. Having served as vice president of programs at the Women's Media Center and executive director of WAM, I'd always been impressed by her beaming white smile and exuberant energy.

In July 2019, we met one-on-one at her office inside CUNY's headquarters on the bustling corner of 34th Street and Fifth Avenue. As we walked into her office, graced with shelves upon shelves of books, I took note of a large black-and-white banner hanging on the back wall emblazoned with the words: HUNDREDS OF BOOKS UNDER MY SKIN. Just above it hung a circular sign paying homage to the power of literature: "She is too fond of books, and it has turned her brain. —Louisa May Alcott (1873)."

Jamia describes herself as a feminist media activist, content creator, organizer, and curator, but most of all a storyteller. I came to the interview prepared to hear her story—about what led her to undertake this role and why. Her black hair was tied up in a bun, and her clothing, composed of a loose-fitting beige top and flowing black pants, made her appear youthful and relaxed. *She could easily be mistaken for a college student herself,* I thought. She sat down in a tall black chair behind a large wooden desk. I sat opposite her on a soft long couch. As I leaned back, I felt relaxed as well. Surrounded by feminist books stacked on her bookshelves—*But Some of Us Are Brave, A Brighter Coming Day*, and *Challenging Racism and Sexism*, all published by The Feminist Press—I was completely at home.

"I am in this position to help change the face of publishing so that it is as diverse as the communities we live in, and that it represents the fullness of who we are," Jamia said in response to my question about her mission as The Feminist Press's relatively new publisher. I looked at the stacks of manuscripts on her desk, some marked with notes, others that looked like they hadn't been tackled just yet.

I related my condolences on her mom's death, which had occurred only eight months earlier. Since her mother's passing, it had been hard on Jamia, understandably. An only child, Jamia reflected on some of the things she'd learned most from her, particularly how she was taught the importance of liberation, both of race and gender, and instilled in her the importance of helping others from an early age.

"I called her the 'Encourager in Chief,'" Jamia told me, referring to her mother's dedication to ensuring that her daughter felt empowered to be anything she wanted from an early age. When it came to buying dolls, her mother wanted Jamia to see herself reflected in them. "She bought me Barbie dolls, but not just any kind. I had the first presidential Barbie, the first multicultural Barbie, and a slew of Cabbage Patch Kids with brown skin."

And when Jamia was honored by Women's eNews as one of our 21 Leaders for the 21st Century in 2018, she was also given the option to select a Barbie from Mattel's recently released Inspiring Women's Series. Jamia chose Officer Lt. Uhura of the television series *Star Trek,* a strong female character who broke ground as one of the first intelligent, trusted, and respected African American women on television.

"Lieutenant Uhura, just like my mom, was a badass," Jamia said boldly, her eyes looking even more intent and focused.

And then there were the birthday cakes. "She made sure that my birthday cakes all had chocolate-brown frosting, which I think was a little *too* intentional," Jamia said, laughing loudly. Still, Jamia is grateful that, as a child, her mom made her aware that Thanksgiving wasn't all it was cracked up to be. She taught her early on that there were inequities that resulted from the pilgrims inflicting pain on Native Americans.

"While other people were still connecting the dots, my mom's teachings had me already there, and I understood it immediately," she recalled proudly. "But this wasn't about censoring the information she provided to me. It was about exposing me to truths about what really occurred. And I still very much feel her presence in that way."

The importance of helping others was also paramount in her family. "It was always about what I am going to do for others . . . always," Jamia recalled. And by leading The Feminist Press, she's now in a strong position to do just that.

"I really connected to joining The Feminist Press at this time," she told me. "My mom read many of their books to me when I was growing up. It shaped my identity as a black woman, but also as an artist, a writer, and a creator," she said. "I am now in a position to honor those voices that helped pave the way for mine and to do so for a whole generation of new writers."

Working alongside the press's founders and board members, some of whom are in their nineties, as well as some of their younger assistants and even teenage interns, demonstrates to Jamia the power of multigenerational learning. "I was born at a different time," Jamia, who is in her late thirties, said. "I didn't experience the Kent State shootings or the gender justice and black power movements of the sixties and seventies, but I understand how movements work, and we are witnessing another one right now." She gave me a firm look and concluded, "The actions we take now will have an effect on the next one hundred years."

As The Feminist Press is gearing up for its fiftieth anniversary celebration in 2020, Jamia noted that the organization is excited to "do the work we do best, which is to create a more just world that everyone can recognize themselves in." This is being done by doubling down on the press's mission to amplify the most marginalized and insurgent voices.

"The work we can do to upload these voices is extremely critical now," Jamia contended. As a springboard for diverse women authors, Jamia also understands that The Feminist Press can inspire movements, which includes purposely promoting trans and gender-nonconforming authors. Speaking to this topic, she rose from her chair and walked over to one of her bookshelves, pulling out a paperback book sporting a hot pink cover and entitled, *Original Plumbing, The Best of 10 Years of Trans Male Culture.* From 2009 to 2019, *Original Plumbing* magazine grew to a nationally acclaimed print quarterly dedicated to trans men, and Jamia told me how proud The Feminist Press had been to publish a book showcasing its very best content earlier that year. She had received a number of letters, in fact, from trans men thanking her for publishing this book because they were able to see themselves in these stories. "They told me that books like these matter to them. And that's just one example of the magic of The Feminist Press. We are changing the face of publishing," Jamia adds proudly.

As for the future, the press is looking forward to continuing to reflect upon what book publishing needs now so that it can expand its reach, ensuring that it will continue to grow for another fifty years. For Jamia, however, the press's success will hinge on more than just its strategic plan. Its mission, after all, emanates from the roots of her childhood. "The message I always received from my mom was to maintain humility and help the community. To take the gifts I was given, and to help other people," Jamia reflected. She recalled that her mother told her, "You are entrusted with this mission when things are challenging, as well as when things are good. With as much as you have been given, so much is expected." Seeing her in her office, listening to her articulate her vision for the press, I imagine that there's no one better suited than Jamia to carry the Feminist Press and its mission forward into the future.

EPILOGUE

While speaking at an event on leadership in December 2019, former US President Barak Obama envisioned what a world run by women would be like: "If women ran every country in the world, there would be a general improvement in living standards and outcomes. They are indisputably better than men, and most problems in the world came from old people, mostly men, holding onto positions of power. I'm absolutely confident that if, for two years, every nation on earth was run by women, you would see a significant improvement across the board on just about everything, living standards and outcomes."

President Obama's foretelling of a better world run by women is already being demonstrated. In addition to the pioneering and pervasive contributions each of this book's thirty interviewees have already accomplished, here is just a sampling of the achievements of female world leaders in the past few months:

In December 2019, Iceland's prime minister, Katrin Jakobssdottir, called for prioritizing environmental and social factors in their budgets over gross domestic product. "We need an alternative future based on wellbeing and inclusive growth," she said.

Earlier that year, when New Zealand was victimized by a terrorist attack in Christchurch, taking the lives of fifty people, Prime Minister Jacinda Ardern enacted immediate and sweeping changes to the country's gun laws by banning all assault rifles and military-style semiautomatic weapons, while also modeling how a compassionate head of state leads. The very next day, she wore a black head scarf in solidarity with Muslim leaders. During her meeting with them, rather than telling them what she planned to do to help her country heal, she asked them what they would like her to do. She also refused to name Islamophobia as the cause of the massacre, minimizing the potential for increased discrimination.

New Zealand and Iceland are both members of the Wellbeing Economy Alliance, a network of countries that are developing frameworks to measure social, economic, and environmental factors in a way that allows countries to prioritize mental health, domestic violence, and child poverty instead of GDP, which has long been considered the sole measure of a country's success.

In Finland, Sanna Marin, who was also elected prime minister in December 2019, instituted a government where the leaders of all five parts are women. Further, by making quality of life a priority, she recently proposed a four-day workweek and a six-hour workday. "Why couldn't it be the next step?" she asked. "I believe people deserve to spend more time with their families, loved ones, hobbies, and other aspects of life, such as culture. This could be the next step for us in working life."

In March 2019, Slovakia elected its first female president, Zuzana Caputova. A former environmental activist, she vowed not only to fight impunity in a country where large-scale political corruption exists, but she's also making environmental protection a priority.

And in Greece, Katerina Sakellaropoulou was elected that country's first female president on January 22, 2020. She has also made saving the environment her mission. She was the former chair of the Hellenic Society for Environmental Law since 2015 and the recipient of the 2016 Goldman Environmental Prize, awarded annually to grassroots environmental activists.

The commitment of female leaders to building a better world is not restricted to these countries, however. According to a 2019 study by Astghik Mavisakalyan, an economics professor at Australia's Curtin University who recently examined the legislatures of ninety-one countries, the larger the percentage of seats held by women, the stronger each country's climate policies. Further, her study found that a higher representation of females in parliament results in lower carbon dioxide emissions. She concluded that female political representation may be an underutilized tool for addressing climate change.

All of this confirms and validates the sentiment expressed by Ambassador Swanee Hunt, one of the thirty interviewees in this book, in her June 2019 political op-ed entitled "What Happens When Women Rule." Citing Nevada, which became the first US state with a majority female legislature (52 percent), and Colorado, second to Nevada with 47 percent women, Swanee pointed out that Nevada passed the Trust Nevada Women Act, which removed criminal penalties for abortions and other barriers to reproductive healthcare. And in Colorado, a bill was passed to move the state toward paid family leave, and a new plan was developed to reduce greenhouse gases.

"It turns out the [glass] ceiling was in our heads," Swanee wrote. "We are now feeling the earth move under our feet."

ABOUT THE AUTHOR

L ori Sokol, PhD, currently serves as the executive director and editor-in-chief of Women's eNews, a nonprofit news organization that reports on the most crucial issues impacting women and girls around the world. As an entrepreneur, scholar, journalist, and psychologist, Dr. Sokol's career spans over thirty-five years of reporting, writing, researching, and publishing on such pertinent social issues as gender equality, the needs of working parents, environmental sustainability, and strides made by female professionals determined to smash the proverbial "glass ceiling." As a doctoral candidate in Educational Psychology, Dr. Sokol's research specifically focused on the media's influence in crafting gender roles, further seeking to expose how stereotypes are created and maintained. She has published academic articles on psychology and the media, and served as an adjunct professor in the Psychology Departments of a number of colleges and universities. Dr. Sokol has also served as a speaker at numerous global women's conferences throughout the United States and Asia on topics related to gender equality and human rights. Her articles have been published in the *Baltimore Sun, The Huffington Post, Ms. Magazine,* and in Slate.com, and she has been profiled in a variety of major publications, most recently in *The Wall Street Journal* and on Forbes.com. She has also been interviewed on MSNBC, CNBC, WPIX, NY1 and Fox Five Live. Her first book, *Flex Primer for the New Future of Work,* was published by Working Mother Media in 2011.

Lori Sokol is also the proud parent of adult children, Jason and Rebecca, whom she considers her proudest achievements.

Author photo © Eva Mueller

SELECTED TITLES FROM SHE WRITES PRESS

She Writes Press is an independent publishing company founded to serve women writers everywhere. Visit us at www.shewritespress.com.

Screwnomics: How Our Economy Works Against Women and Real Ways to Make Lasting Change by Rickey Gard Diamond. $16.95, 978-1-63152-318-2. Reaching back from the most recent economic crash to ancient times, Screwnomics explains the underlying sexual history of today's economics and issues a clarion call for today's women to join what has been a nearly exclusively male conversation for the past 2,500 years.

Love Her, Love Her Not: The Hillary Paradox edited by Joanne Bamberger. $16.95, 978-1-63152-806-4. A collection of personal essays by noted women essayists and emerging women writers that explores the question of why Americans have a love/hate "relationship" with Hillary Clinton.

Transforming Knowledge: Public Talks on Women's Studies, 1976-2011 by Jean Fox O'Barr. $19.95, 978-1-938314-48-3. A collection of essays addressing one woman's challenges faced and lessons learned on the path to reframing—and effecting—feminist change.

100 Under $100: One Hundred Tools for Empowering Global Women by Betsy Teutsch. $29.95, 978-1-63152-934-4. An inspiring, comprehensive look at the many tools being employed today to empower women in the developing world and help them raise themselves out of poverty.

Stop Giving it Away: How to Stop Self-Sacrificing and Start Claiming Your Space, Power, and Happiness by Cherilynn Veland. $16.95, 978-1-63152-958-0. An empowering guide designed to help women break free from the trappings of the needs, wants, and whims of other people—and the self-imposed limitations that are keeping them from happiness.

Drop In: Lead with Deeper Presence and Courage by Sara Harvey Yao. $14.95, 978-1-63152-161-4. A compelling explanation about why being present is so challenging and how leaders can access clarity, connection, and courage in the midst of their chaotic lives, inside and outside of work.

CPSIA information can be obtained
at www.ICGtesting.com
Printed in the USA
JSHW040717270721
17271JS00002B/5

9 781631 527159